D0234734

JARON LANIER

Jaron Lanier is one of the most celebrated pioneers of digital innovation in the world, and also one of the earliest and most prescient critics of its current trajectory. His previous books include the international bestsellers *Who Owns the Future?* and *You Are Not a Gadget,* both chosen as best books of the year by the *New York Times*, and most recently *Dawn of the New Everything: A Journey Through Virtual Reality,* chosen as a best book of the year by the *Wall Street Journal, The Economist* and *Vox.* He was named one of the 100 most influential people in the world by *Time,* one of the 100 top public intellectuals by *Foreign Policy,* and one of the top 50 World Thinkers by *Prospect.*

ALSO BY JARON LANIER

Dawn of the New Everything
Who Owns the Future?
You Are Not a Gadget: A Manifesto
Wenn Träume *erwachsen warden (When Dreams Grow Up)*

JARON LANIER

Ten Arguments for Deleting Your Social Media Accounts Right Now

VINTAGE

1 3 5 7 9 10 8 6 4 2

Vintage
20 Vauxhall Bridge Road,
London SW1V 2SA

Vintage is part of the Penguin Random House group of companies
whose addresses can be found at global.penguinrandomhouse.com.

Penguin
Random House
UK

First published in the UK by The Bodley Head in 2018
First published by Vintage in 2019

penguin.co.uk/vintage

A CIP catalogue record for this book is available from the British Library

ISBN 9781529112405

Printed and bound by Clays Ltd, Elcograf S.p.A.

Penguin Random House is committed to a sustainable future
for our business, our readers and our planet. This book is
made from Forest Stewardship Council® certified paper.

MIX
Paper from
responsible sources
FSC® C018179

CONTENTS

ARGUMENT NINE

SOCIAL MEDIA IS MAKING
POLITICS IMPOSSIBLE

ARGUMENT TEN

SOCIAL MEDIA HATES YOUR SOUL

CONCLUSION: CATS HAVE NINE LIVES

TEN ARGUMENTS FOR DELETING YOUR SOCIAL MEDIA ACCOUNTS RIGHT NOW

INTRODUCTION, WITH CATS

Let's start with cats.

Cats are everywhere online. They make the memiest memes and the cutest videos.

Why cats more than dogs?[1]

Dogs didn't come to ancient humans begging to live with us; we domesticated them.[2] They've been bred to be obedient. They take to training and they are predictable. They work for us. That's not to say anything against dogs.[3] It's great that they're loyal and dependable.

Cats are different. They came along and partly domesticated themselves. They are not predictable. Popular dog videos tend to show off training, while the most wildly popular

---

[1] http://www.movingimage.us/exhibitions/2015/08/07/detail/how-cats-took-over -the-internet/

[2] https://www.smithsonianmag.com/smithsonian-institution/ask-smithsonian-are -cats-domesticated-180955111/

[3] Peace, dog lovers! Here's a speculation that dogs domesticated themselves, like cats: https://news.nationalgeographic.com/news/2013/03/130302-dog-domestic -evolution-science-wolf-wolves-human/.

cat videos are the ones that capture weird and surprising behaviors.

Cats are smart, but not a great choice if you want an animal that takes to training reliably. Watch a cat circus online, and what's so touching is that the cats are clearly making their own minds up about whether to do a trick they've learned, or to do nothing, or to wander into the audience.

Cats have done the seemingly impossible: They've integrated themselves into the modern high-tech world without giving themselves up. They are still in charge. There is no worry that some stealthy meme crafted by algorithms and paid for by a creepy, hidden oligarch has taken over your cat. No one has taken over your cat; not you, not anyone.

Oh, how we long to have that certainty not just about our cats, but about ourselves! Cats on the internet are our hopes and dreams for the future of people on the internet.

Meanwhile, even though we love dogs, we don't want to *be* dogs, at least in terms of power relationships with people, and we're afraid Facebook and the like are turning us into dogs. When we are triggered to do something crappy online, we might call it a response to a "dog whistle." Dog whistles can only be heard by dogs. We worry that we're falling under stealthy control.

This book is about how to be a cat. How can you remain autonomous in a world where you are under constant surveillance and are constantly prodded by algorithms run by some of the richest corporations in history, which have no way of making money except by being paid to manipulate your behavior? How can you be a cat, despite that?

The title doesn't lie; this book presents ten arguments for deleting all your social media accounts. I hope it helps, but even if you agree with all ten of my arguments, you might still decide to keep some of your accounts. That's part of your prerogative, being a cat.

As I present the ten arguments, I'll discuss some of the ways you might think about your situation to decide what's best for you. But only you can know.

AUTHOR'S NOTE, MARCH 2018:

This book was written primarily during the final months of 2017, but events in 2018 turned out to be explosively relevant. The manuscript was done, done, done—headed to the printer—when the sorry revelations of the Cambridge Analytica scandal fueled a sudden, grassroots movement of people deleting Facebook accounts.

Unfortunately, not all public figures and thought leaders handled the moment with the courage that was required. There were pundits who tried to quit but could not. There were others who pointed out that not everyone is privileged enough to quit, so it felt cruel to leave the less fortunate behind. Others said it was irrelevant to quit because the thing that mattered was pressuring governments to regulate Facebook. Overall, the attitude of professional commentators regarding account deleters was smug and dismissive. And dead wrong.

C'mon people! Yes, being able to quit is a privilege; many genuinely can't. But if you have the latitude to quit and don't, you are not supporting the less fortunate; you are only reinforcing the system in which many people are trapped. I am living proof that you can have a public life in media without social media accounts. Those of us with options must explore those options or they will remain only theoretical. Business follows money, so we who have options have power and responsibility. You, you, you have the affirmative responsibility to invent and demonstrate ways to live without the crap that is destroying society. Quitting is the only way, for now, to learn what can replace our grand mistake.

YOU ARE LOSING YOUR
FREE WILL

WELCOME TO THE CAGE THAT GOES
EVERYWHERE WITH YOU

Something entirely new is happening in the world. Just in the last five or ten years, nearly everyone started to carry a little device called a smartphone on their person all the time that's suitable for algorithmic behavior modification. A lot of us are also using related devices called smart speakers on our kitchen counters or in our car dashboards. We're being tracked and measured constantly, and receiving engineered feedback all the time. We're being hypnotized little by little by technicians we can't see, for purposes we don't know. We're all lab animals now.

Algorithms gorge on data about you, every second. What kinds of links do you click on? What videos do you watch all the way through? How quickly are you moving from one thing to the next? Where are you when you do these things? Who are you connecting with in person and online? What facial expressions do you make? How does your skin tone change in different situations? What were you doing just before you decided to buy something or not? Whether to vote or not?

All these measurements and many others have been matched up with similar readings about the lives of multitudes of other people through massive spying. Algorithms correlate what you do with what almost everyone else has done.

The algorithms don't really understand you, but there is power in numbers, especially in large numbers. If a lot of other people who like the foods you like were also more easily put off by pictures of a candidate portrayed in a pink border instead of a blue one, then you *probably* will be too, and no one needs to know why. Statistics are reliable, but only as idiot demons.

Are you sad, lonely, scared? Happy, confident? Getting your period? Experiencing a peak of class anxiety?

So-called advertisers can seize the moment when you are perfectly primed and then influence you with messages that have worked on other people who share traits and situations with you.

I say "so-called" because it's just not right to call direct manipulation of people advertising. Advertisers used to have a limited chance to make a pitch, and that pitch might have been sneaky or annoying, but it was fleeting. Furthermore, lots of people saw the same TV or print ad; it wasn't adapted to individuals. The biggest difference was that you weren't monitored and assessed all the time so that you could be fed dynamically optimized stimuli—whether "content" or ad—to engage and alter you.

Now everyone who is on social media is getting individualized, continuously adjusted stimuli, without a break, so long as they use their smartphones. What might once have been called advertising must now be understood as continuous behavior modification on a titanic scale.

Please don't be insulted. Yes, I am suggesting that you might be turning, just a little, into a well-trained dog, or something less pleasant, like a lab rat or a robot. That you're being remote-controlled, just a little, by clients of big corporations. But if I'm right, then becoming aware of it might just free you, so give this a chance, okay?

A scientific movement called behaviorism arose before computers were invented. Behaviorists studied new, more methodical, sterile, and nerdy ways to train animals and humans.

One famous behaviorist was B. F. Skinner. He set up a methodical system, known as a Skinner box, in which caged animals got treats when they did something specific. There wasn't anyone petting or whispering to the animal, just a purely isolated mechanical action—a new kind of training for modern times. Various behaviorists, who often gave off rather ominous vibes, applied this method to people. Behaviorist strategies often worked, which freaked everyone out, eventually leading to a bunch of creepy "mind control" sci-fi and horror movie scripts.

An unfortunate fact is that you can train someone using behaviorist techniques, *and the person doesn't even know it*. Until very recently, this rarely happened unless you signed up to be a test subject in an experiment in the basement of a university's psychology building. Then you'd go into a room and be tested while someone watched you through a one-way mirror. Even though you knew an experiment was going on, you didn't realize *how* you were being manipulated. At least you gave consent to be manipulated in *some* way. (Well, not always. There were all kinds of cruel experiments performed on prisoners, on poor people, and especially on racial targets.)

This book argues in ten ways that what has become suddenly normal—pervasive surveillance and constant, subtle manipulation—is unethical, cruel, dangerous, and inhumane.

Dangerous? Oh, yes, because who knows who's going to use that power, and for what?

THE MAD SCIENTIST TURNS OUT TO CARE ABOUT THE DOG IN THE CAGE

You may have heard the mournful confessions from the founders of social media empires, which I prefer to call "behavior modification empires."

Here's Sean Parker, the first president of Facebook:

> We need to sort of give you a little dopamine hit every once in a while, because someone liked or commented on a photo or a post or whatever. . . . It's a social-validation feedback loop . . . exactly the kind of thing that a hacker like myself would come up with, because you're exploiting a vulnerability in human psychology. . . . The inventors, creators—it's me, it's Mark [Zuckerberg], it's Kevin Systrom on Instagram, it's all of these people—understood this consciously. And we did it anyway . . . it literally changes your relationship with society, with each other. . . . It probably interferes with productivity in weird ways. God only knows what it's doing to our children's brains.[1]

Here's Chamath Palihapitiya, former vice president of user growth at Facebook:

> The short-term, dopamine-driven feedback loops we've created are destroying how society works. . . . No civil discourse, no cooperation; misinformation, mistruth. And it's not an American problem—this is not about Russian ads. This is a

[1] https://www.axios.com/sean-parker-unloads-on-facebook-2508036343.html

global problem. . . . I feel tremendous guilt. I think we all knew in the back of our minds—even though we feigned this whole line of, like, there probably aren't any bad unintended consequences. I think in the back, deep, deep recesses of, we kind of knew something bad could happen. . . . So we are in a really bad state of affairs right now, in my opinion. It is erod-ing the core foundation of how people behave by and between each other. And I don't have a good solution. My solution is I just don't use these tools anymore. I haven't for years.[2]

Better late than never. Plenty of critics like me have been warning that bad stuff was happening for a while now, but to hear this from the people who did the stuff is progress, a step forward.

For years, I had to endure quite painful criticism from friends in Silicon Valley because I was perceived as a traitor for criticiz-ing what we were doing. Lately I have the opposite problem. I argue that Silicon Valley people are for the most part decent, and I ask that we not be villainized; I take a lot of fresh heat for that. Whether I've been too hard or too soft on my com-munity is hard to know.

The more important question now is whether anyone's crit-icism will matter. It's undeniably out in the open that a bad technology is doing us harm, but will we —will you, mean-ing *you*—be able to resist and help steer the world to a better place?

Companies like Facebook, Google, and Twitter are finally trying to fix some of the massive problems they created, albeit in a piecemeal way. Is it because they are being pressured or

---

[2] https://gizmodo.com/former-facebook-exec-you-don-t-realize-it-but-you-are -1821181133. Though I must note that Palihapitiya walked back his statement a bit in the following days, talking about how he thought Facebook did good overall in the world.

because they feel that it's the right thing to do? Probably a little of both.

The companies are changing policies, hiring humans to monitor what's going on, and hiring data scientists to come up with algorithms to avoid the worst failings. Facebook's old mantra was "Move fast and break things,"[3] and now they're coming up with better mantras and picking up a few pieces from a shattered world and gluing them together.

This book will argue that the companies on their own can't do enough to glue the world back together.

Because people in Silicon Valley are expressing regrets, you might think that now you just need to wait for us to fix the problem. That's not how things work. If you aren't part of the solution, there will be no solution.

This first argument will introduce a few key concepts behind the design of addictive and manipulative network services. Awareness is the first step to freedom.

CARROT AND SHTICK

Parker says Facebook intentionally got people addicted, while Palihapitiya is saying something about the negative effects on relationships and society. What is the connection between these two mea culpas?

The core process that allows social media to make money and that also does the damage to society is *behavior modification*. Behavior modification entails methodical techniques that change behavioral patterns in animals and people. It can be used to treat addictions, but it can also be used to create them.

The damage to society comes because addiction makes

---

[3] https://mashable.com/2014/04/30/facebooks-new-mantra-move-fast-with
  -stability/

people crazy. The addict gradually loses touch with the real world and real people. When many people are addicted to manipulative schemes, the world gets dark and crazy.

Addiction is a neurological process that we don't understand completely. The neurotransmitter dopamine plays a role in pleasure and is thought to be central to the mechanism of behavior change in response to getting rewards. That is why Parker brings it up.

Behavior modification, especially the modern kind implemented with gadgets like smartphones, is a statistical effect, meaning it's real but not comprehensively reliable; over a population, the effect is more or less predictable, but for each individual it's impossible to say. *To a degree*, you're an animal in a behaviorist's experimental cage. But the fact that something is fuzzy or approximate does not make it unreal.

Originally, food treats were the most common reward used in behaviorist experiments, though the practice goes back to ancient times. Every animal trainer uses them, slipping a little treat to a dog after it has performed a trick. Many parents of young children do it, too.

One of the first behaviorists, Ivan Pavlov, famously demonstrated that he didn't need to use real food. He would ring a bell when a dog was fed, and eventually the dog would salivate upon hearing the bell alone.

Using symbols instead of real rewards has become an essential trick in the behavior modification toolbox. For instance, a smartphone game like Candy Crush uses shiny images of candy instead of real candy to become addictive. Other addictive video games might use shiny images of coins or other treasure.

Addictive pleasure and reward patterns in the brain—the "little dopamine hit" cited by Sean Parker—are part of the basis of social media addiction, but not the whole story, because social media also uses punishment and negative reinforcement.

Various kinds of punishment have been used in behaviorist labs; electric shocks were popular for a while. But just as with rewards, it's not necessary for punishments to be real and physical. Sometimes experiments deny a subject points or tokens.

You are getting the equivalent of both treats *and* electric shocks when you use social media.

Most users of social media have experienced catfishing[4] (which cats hate), senseless rejection, being belittled or ignored, outright sadism, or all of the above, and worse. Just as the carrot and stick work together, unpleasant feedback can play as much of a role in addiction and sneaky behavior modification as the pleasant kind.

THE ALLURE OF MYSTERY

When Parker uses the phrase "every once in a while," he's probably referring to one of the curious phenomena that behaviorists discovered while studying both animals and people. If someone gets a reward—whether it's positive social regard or a piece of candy—whenever they do a particular thing, then they'll tend to do more of that thing. When people get a flattering response in exchange for posting something on social media, they get in the habit of posting more.

That sounds innocent enough, but it can be the first stage of an addiction that becomes a problem both for individuals and society. Even though Silicon Valley types have a sanitized name for this phase, "engagement," we fear it enough to keep our own children away from it. Many of the Silicon Valley kids I know attend Waldorf schools, which generally forbid electronics.

Back to the surprising phenomenon: it's not that positive

---

[4] https://en.wikipedia.org/wiki/Catfishing

and negative feedback work, but that somewhat random or unpredictable feedback can be more engaging than perfect feedback.

If you get a piece of candy immediately every time you say please as a child, you'll probably start saying please more often. But suppose once in a while the candy doesn't come. You might guess that you'd start saying please less often. After all, it's not generating the reward as reliably as it used to.

But sometimes the opposite thing happens. It's as if your brain, a born pattern finder, can't resist the challenge. "There must be some additional trick to it," murmurs your obsessive brain. You keep on pleasing, hoping that a deeper pattern will reveal itself, even though there's nothing but bottomless randomness.

It's healthy for a scientist to be fascinated by a pattern that doesn't quite make sense. Maybe that means there's something deeper to be discovered. And it's a great tool to exploit if you're writing a script. A little incongruity makes a plot or a character more fascinating.

But in many situations it's a *terrible* basis for fascination. The allure of glitchy feedback is probably what draws a lot of people into crummy "codependent" relationships in which they aren't treated well.

A touch of randomness is more than easy to generate in social media: because the algorithms aren't perfect, randomness is intrinsic. But beyond that, feeds are usually calculated to include an additional degree of intentional randomness. The motivation originally came from basic math, not human psychology.

Social media algorithms are usually "adaptive," which means they constantly make small changes to themselves in order to try to get better results; "better" in this case meaning more engaging and therefore more profitable. A little randomness is always present in this type of algorithm.

Let's suppose an algorithm is showing you an opportunity to buy socks or stocks about five seconds after you see a cat video that makes you happy. An adaptive algorithm will occasionally perform an automatic test to find out what happens if the interval is changed to, say, four and a half seconds. Did that make you more likely to buy? If so, that timing adjustment might be applied not only to your future feed, but to the feeds of thousands of other people who seem correlated with you because of anything from color preferences to driving patterns.[5]

Adaptive algorithms can get stuck sometimes; if an algorithm gets no further benefits from further small tweaks to its settings, then further small tweaks won't stick. If changing to four and a half seconds makes you *less* likely to buy socks, but five and a half seconds *also* makes sales less likely, then the timing will remain at five seconds. On the basis of available evidence, five seconds would be the best possible time to wait. If no small random change helps, then the algorithm stops adapting. But adaptive algorithms aren't supposed to stop adapting.

Suppose changing even more might improve the result? Maybe two and a half seconds would be better, for instance. But incremental tweaks wouldn't reveal that, because the algorithm got stuck at the five-second setting. That's why adaptive algorithms *also* often include a sparser dose of greater randomness. Every once in while an algorithm finds better settings by being jarred out of merely okay settings.[6]

---

[5] The optimization of timing is only one example out of many. *Every* design choice in your social media experiences is being optimized all the time on similar principles. Ex-Googler Tristan Harris has assembled more examples, including the way options of all kinds are shown to you, the way you are able to click on options, and the ways that you and others are shown options in tandem. Look for his essays, including "How Technology Hijacks People's Minds," at http://www.tristanharris.com/.

[6] Mathematicians often think of this process as crawling around on an imaginary "energy landscape." Each position on the energy landscape corresponds to a setting for parameters that might change, so as you metaphorically crawl on the landscape you are exploring different parameter settings. The five-second mark would

Adaptive systems often include such a leaping mechanism. An example is the occurrence of useful mutations in natural evolution, which is usually animated by more incremental selection-based events in which the genes from an individual are either passed along or not. A mutation is a wild card that adds new possibilities, a jarring jump. Every once in a while a mutation adds a weird, new, and enhancing feature to a species.

Neuroscientists naturally wonder whether a similar process is happening within the human brain. Our brains surely include adaptive processes; brains might be adapted to seek out surprises, because nature abhors a rut.

When an algorithm is feeding experiences to a person, it turns out that the randomness that lubricates algorithmic adaptation can also feed human addiction. The algorithm is trying to capture the perfect parameters for manipulating a brain, while the brain, in order to seek out deeper meaning, is changing in response to the algorithm's experiments; it's a cat-and-mouse game based on pure math. Because the stimuli from the algorithm don't mean anything, because they genuinely are random, the brain isn't adapting to anything real, but to a fiction. That process—of becoming hooked on an elusive mirage—*is* addiction. As the algorithm tries to escape a rut, the human mind becomes stuck in one.

The pioneers of the online exploitation of this intersection of math and the human brain were not the social media companies, but the creators of digital gambling machines like video poker, and then of online gambling sites. Occasionally, pioneers

---

correspond to a valley that the algorithm has settled into. Deeper is better in this visualization, because it takes less energy to be deeper, or you could think of the metaphor as digging deeper into buried gold deposits. Within this thought world, the two-and-a-half-second setting is a deeper valley that you'd never find by taking small steps from the bottom of the five-second valley, because you always slide back. The only way to find the deeper valley is by being forced to make a big speculative leap.

of the gambling world complain about how social media companies ripped off their ideas and made more money, but mostly they talk about how social media is helping them identify the easiest marks.[7]

HEAVEN AND HELL ARE MADE OF OTHER PEOPLE[8]

Social networks bring in another dimension of stimuli: social pressure.

People are keenly sensitive to social status, judgment, and competition. Unlike most animals, people are not only born absolutely helpless, but also remain so for years. We only survive by getting along with family members and others. Social concerns are not optional features of the human brain. They are primal.

The power of what other people think has proven to be intense enough to modify the behavior of subjects participating in famous studies like the Milgram Experiment and the Stanford Prison Experiment. Normal, noncriminal people were coerced into doing horrible things, such as torturing others, through no mechanism other than social pressure.

On social networks, the manipulation of social emotions has been the easiest way to generate rewards and punishments. That might change someday, if drones start dropping actual candy from the sky when you do what the algorithm wants, but for now it's all about feelings that can be evoked in you—mostly, feelings regarding what other people think.

For instance, when we are afraid that we might not be

---

[7] https://link.springer.com/article/10.1007%2Fs10899-015-9525-2
[8] This is a reference to a play by Jean-Paul Sartre; look it up!

considered cool, attractive, or high-status, we don't feel good. That fear is a profound emotion. It hurts.[9]

Everybody suffers from social anxiety from time to time, and every child has encountered a bully who used social anxiety as a weapon of torture, probably because behaving like a bully lessened the chances that the bully might become a target. That's why people, even those who would normally be decent, tend to pile on to a victim of social anxiety torture. They're so afraid of the very real pain that social anxiety brings that they can lose sight of their better natures for a moment.

That's not to say that all social emotions are negative. We can also experience camaraderie, sympathy, respect, admiration, gratitude, hope, empathy, closeness, attraction, and a world of other positive feelings when we interact with other people. On the negative side, we might feel fear, hostility, anxiety, resentment, repulsion, jealousy, and a desire to ridicule.

If socially evoked emotion can function as punishment or reward, then is reward or punishment more effective at changing people? This question has been studied for a long time, and it seems that the answer varies according to the population being studied and the situation. Here's a study that suggests that young children respond better to reward than punishment, though the reverse might be the case after age twelve.[10] Here's another study that suggests that punishment is more effective than reward for manipulating college students.[11] Here's a summary of research indicating that affirmation works better to motivate adult workers.[12] It might be that the nature of the

[9] http://people.hss.caltech.edu/~lyariv/papers/DarkSide1.pdf

[10] http://esciencenews.com/articles/2008/09/25/from.12.years.onward.you.learn.differently

[11] https://source.wustl.edu/2015/05/carrot-or-stick-punishments-may-guide-behavior-more-effectively-than-rewards/

[12] https://hbr.org/2017/09/what-motivates-employees-more-rewards-or-punishments

task determines which type of feedback is more effective,[13] as does the way the task is described.[14]

A corpus of academic research compares the powers of positive and negative feedback, but that is not the key question for the design of commercial social media platforms, which are primarily concerned with reducing costs and increasing performance, thereby maximizing profit. Whether or not positive feedback might in theory be more effective in certain cases, negative feedback turns out to be the *bargain* feedback, the best choice for business, so it appears more often in social media.

Negative emotions such as fear and anger well up more easily and dwell in us longer than positive ones. It takes longer to build trust than to lose trust. Fight-or-flight responses occur in seconds, while it can take hours to relax.

This is true in real life, but it is even more true in the flattened light of algorithms.

There is no evil genius seated in a cubicle in a social media company performing calculations and deciding that making people feel bad is more "engaging" and therefore more profitable than making them feel good. Or at least, I've never met or heard of such a person.

The prime directive to be engaging reinforces itself, and no one even notices that negative emotions are being amplified more than positive ones. Engagement is not meant to serve any particular purpose other than its own enhancement, and yet the result is an unnatural global amplification of the "easy" emotions, which happen to be the negative ones.

---

[13] http://onlinelibrary.wiley.com/doi/10.1002/job.725/pdf
[14] https://repositories.lib.utexas.edu/handle/2152/24850

BIT AS BAIT

In the bigger picture, in which people must do more than conform in order for our species to thrive, <u>behaviorism is an inadequate way to think about society</u>. *If* you want to motivate high value and creative outcomes, as opposed to undertaking rote training, *then* reward and punishment aren't the right tools at all.

There's a long line of researchers studying this topic, starting with Abraham Maslow in the 1950s and continuing with many others, including Mihaly Csikszentmihalyi (joined by writers like Daniel Pink). Instead of applying the simple mechanisms of behaviorism, we need to think about people in more creative ways, if we expect them to be creative. We need to foster joy, intellectual challenge, individuality, curiosity, and other qualities that don't fit into a tidy chart.

But there's something about the rigidity of digital technology, the on-and-off nature of the bit, that attracts the behaviorist way of thinking. Reward and punishment are like one and zero. It's not surprising that B. F. Skinner was a major player in the earliest days of digital networking, for instance.[15] He saw digital networks as an ideal way to train a population for the kind of utopia he sought, where we'd all just finally behave. One of his books was called *Beyond Freedom and Dignity*. Beyond!

The term "engagement" is part of the familiar, sanitized language that hides how stupid a machine we have built. We must start using terms like "addiction" and "behavior modification." Here's another example of sanitized language: We *still* call the customers of social media companies "advertisers"— and, to be fair, many of them are. They want you to buy a particular brand of soap or something. But they might also be

---

[15] http://friendlyorangeglow.com/

nasty, hidden creeps who want to undermine democracy. So I prefer to call this class of person a manipulator.

Sorry, soap sellers. . . . Actually, I can report, the people at companies like Procter & Gamble are just fine—I've met a bunch of them—and their world would be happier if they weren't beholden to social media companies.

Back in its earliest days, online advertising really was just advertising. But before long, advances in computing happened to coincide with ridiculously perverse financial incentives, as will be explained in the next argument. What started as advertising morphed into what would better be called "empires of behavior modification for rent." That transformation has often attracted new kinds of customers/manipulators, and they aren't pretty.

Unfortunately, manipulators can't get any result they want with equal ease. You can't pay social media companies to help end wars and make everyone kind. Social media is biased, not to the Left or the Right, but downward. The relative ease of using negative emotions for the purposes of addiction and manipulation makes it relatively easier to achieve undignified results. An unfortunate combination of biology and math favors degradation of the human world. Information warfare units sway elections, hate groups recruit, and nihilists get amazing bang for the buck when they try to bring society down.

The unplanned nature of the transformation from advertising to direct behavior modification caused an explosive amplification of negativity in human affairs. We'll return to the higher potency of negative emotions in behavior modification many times as we explore the personal, political, economic, social, and cultural effects of social media.

ADDICTION, MEET NETWORK EFFECT

Addiction is a big part of the reason why so many of us accept being spied on and manipulated by our information technology, but it's not the only reason. Digital networks genuinely deliver value to us. They allow for great efficiencies and convenience. That's why so many of us worked so hard to make them possible.

Once you can use a pocket device to order rides and food and find out where to meet your friends right away, it's hard to go back. It's hard to remember that people with rare medical conditions used to have no way of finding other people in the same boat, so there was no one to talk to about unusual problems. What a blessing that it has become possible.

But the benefits of networks only appear when people use the same platform. If no one wanted to be an Uber driver, then your Uber app would accomplish exactly nothing. If no one wants to be on your dating app, then, once again, nothing.

The unfortunate result is that once an app starts to work, everyone is stuck with it. It's hard to quit a particular social network and go to a different one, because everyone you know is already on the first one. It's effectively impossible for everyone in a society to back up all their data, move simultaneously, and restore their memories at the same time.

Effects of this kind are called network effects or lock-ins. They're hard to avoid on digital networks.

Originally, many of us who worked on scaling the internet[16] hoped that the thing that would bring people together—that would gain network effect and lock-in—would be the internet

---

[16] "Scaling" is Silicon Valley talk for making something giant. I include myself in the "we" because in the 1990s I used to be the chief scientist of the engineering office of Internet2, the consortium of universities charged with solving the problem of how to make the internet continue to function as it became giant.

itself. But there was a libertarian wind blowing, so we left out many key functions. The internet in itself didn't include a mechanism for personal identity, for instance. Each computer has its own code number, but people aren't represented at all. Similarly, the internet in itself doesn't give you any place to store even a small amount of persistent information, any way to make or receive payments, or any way to find other people you might have something in common with.

Everyone knew that these functions and many others would be needed. We figured it would be wiser to let entrepreneurs fill in the blanks than to leave that task to government. What we didn't consider was that fundamental digital needs like the ones I just listed would lead to new kinds of massive monopolies because of network effects and lock-in. We foolishly laid the foundations for global monopolies. We did their hardest work for them. More precisely, since you're the product, not the customer of social media, the proper word is "monopsonies."[17] Our early libertarian idealism resulted in gargantuan, global data monopsonies.

One of the main reasons to delete your social media accounts is that there isn't a real choice to move to different social media accounts. Quitting entirely is the only option for change. If you don't quit, you are not creating the space in which Silicon Valley can act to improve itself.

---

[17] A monopoly exists when there is only one seller, while a monopsony exists when there is only one buyer. You could say that the iOS and Android smartphone platforms are a duopoly, because they are effectively the only channels for smartphone apps, but you could also say they are a duopsony, because any money that flows into apps has to go through them.

ADDICTION AND FREE WILL
ARE OPPOSITES

Addiction gradually turns you into a zombie. Zombies don't have free will. Once again, this result isn't total but statistical. You become more like a zombie, more of the time, than you otherwise would be.

There's no need to believe in some myth of perfect people who are completely free of addictions. They don't exist. You're not going to become perfect or perfectly free, no matter how many self-help books you read or how many addictive services you quit.

There's no such thing as perfectly free will. Our brains are constantly changing their ways to adapt to a changing environment. It's hard work, and brains get tired! Sometimes they take a break, zone out, and run on autopilot. But that's different from being driven by hidden manipulators.

We modify each other's behavior all the time, and that's a good thing. You'd have to be insensitive and uncaring to not change how you act around someone in response to how that person reacts. When mutual behavior modification gets good, it might be part of what we talk about when we talk about love.

We don't have to think of free will as a supernatural intervention in our universe. Maybe free will exists when our adaptation to each other and the world has an exceptionally creative quality.

So the problem isn't behavior modification in itself. The problem is relentless, robotic, ultimately meaningless behavior modification in the service of unseen manipulators and uncaring algorithms.

Hypnosis might be therapeutic so long as you trust your hypnotist, but who would trust a hypnotist who is working for unknown third parties? Who? Apparently billions of people.

Consider the billions of dollars taken in by Facebook, Google, and the rest of the so-called digital advertising industry every month. The vast majority of that money comes from parties who are seeking to change your behavior, and who believe they are getting results. Many of these behavior changes are similar to the ones that television ads try to provoke, like getting you to buy a car or go to a café.

But, despite in some ways knowing more about you than you know about yourself, the companies don't always know the identities of the advertisers, the parties who are benefiting from manipulating you. Tech company lawyers have testified under oath that the companies couldn't have known when Russian intelligence services sought to disrupt elections or foment divisions to weaken societies, for instance.[18]

I find that paranoid thinking is generally counterproductive. It disempowers you. But consider the present situation. We know that social media has been successfully deployed to disrupt societies,[19] and we know that the price to do so is remarkably low. We know that relevant companies take in an astounding amount of money and that they don't always know who their customers are. Therefore, there are likely to be actors manipulating us—manipulating you—who have not been revealed.

To free yourself, to be more authentic, to be less addicted, to be less manipulated, to be less paranoid . . . for all these marvelous reasons, delete your accounts.

---

[18] https://www.washingtonpost.com/news/the-switch/wp/2017/10/31/facebook
-google-and-twitter-are-set-to-testify-on-capitol-hill-heres-what-to-expect/
[19] https://thestrategybridge.org/the-bridge/2017/5/10/how-russia-weaponized-social
-media-in-crimea

QUITTING SOCIAL MEDIA
IS THE MOST FINELY
TARGETED WAY TO RESIST
THE INSANITY OF OUR TIMES

THE BUMMER MACHINE

It might not seem like it at first, but I'm an optimist. I don't think we have to throw the whole digital world away. A lot of it's great!

The problem isn't the smartphone, as suggested by a flood of articles with titles like "Has the Smartphone Destroyed a Generation?"[1] The problem isn't the internet, which is also routinely accused of ruining the world.[2]

Something *is* ruining the world, but it isn't that we're connecting with people at a distance using bits, or that we're staring into little glowing screens. To be sure, you can overdo staring at the little screen,[3] just as you can overdo a lot of things, but that's not an existential problem for our species.

---

[1] https://www.theatlantic.com/magazine/archive/2017/09/has-the-smartphone
-destroyed-a-generation/534198/

[2] https://bits.blogs.nytimes.com/2011/12/03/how-the-internet-is-destroying
-everything/

[3] http://www.berkeleywellness.com/self-care/preventive-care/article/are-mobile
-devices-ruining-our-eyes

There is one particular high-tech thing, however, that is toxic even in small quantities. One new development that must be quashed. It's important to define the problem as accurately as possible, lest we confuse ourselves even more.

The problem is *in part* that we are all carrying around devices that are suitable for mass behavior modification. But that's not quite the right framing of our problem. After all, our devices can be used for other purposes, and often are.

The problem is not only that users are crammed into online environments that can bring out the worst in us. It's not only that so much power has concentrated into a tiny number of hands that control giant cloud computers.

The problem intersects with all those factors, but even that conglomeration isn't exactly the problem.

The problem occurs when all the phenomena I've just described are driven by a business model in which the incentive is to find customers ready to pay to modify someone else's behavior. Remember, with old-fashioned advertising, you could measure whether a product did better after an ad was run, but now companies are measuring whether *individuals* changed their behaviors, and the feeds for each person are constantly tweaked to get individual behavior to change. Your specific behavior change has been turned into a product. It's a particularly "engaging" product not just for users, but for customers/manipulators, because they worry that if they don't pay up, they'll be left out in the cold.

The problem is *all of the above* plus one more thing. As explained in the first argument, the scheme I am describing amplifies negative emotions more than positive ones, so it's more efficient at harming society than at improving it: creepier customers get more bang for their buck.

Finally, we can draw a circle around the problem. That means we can kill it without collateral damage. Our problem is blessedly specific.

If we could just get rid of the deleterious business model, then the underlying technology might not be so bad. At least, we have to try, because otherwise we'll eventually have to gut a whole universe of digital technology. Tech was the last "god that hadn't failed,"[4] the last bastion of optimism. We can't afford to ditch it.

If you have good experiences with social media, nothing in this book invalidates those experiences. In fact, my hope is that we—meaning both the industry and all of us—will find a way to keep and improve on what we love precisely by being precise about what must be rejected. Deleting your accounts now will improve the chances that you'll have access to better experiences in the future.

Some have compared social media to the tobacco industry,[5] but I will not. The better analogy is paint that contains lead. When it became undeniable that lead was harmful, no one declared that houses should never be painted again. Instead, after pressure and legislation, lead-free paints became the new standard.[6] Smart people simply waited to buy paint until there was a safe version on sale. Similarly, smart people should delete their accounts until nontoxic varieties are available.

I speak as a computer scientist, not as a social scientist or psychologist. From that perspective, I can see that time is running out. The world is changing rapidly under our command, so doing nothing is not an option. We don't have as much in the way of rigorous science as would be ideal for understanding our

[4] https://en.wikipedia.org/wiki/The_God_that_Failed
[5] https://www.forbes.com/sites/elizabethmacbride/2017/12/31/is-social-media-the-tobacco-industry-of-the-21st-century/
[6] https://www.hud.gov/sites/documents/20258_LEGISLATIVEHISTORY.PDF

situation, but we have enough results to describe the problem we must solve, just not a lot of time in which to solve it.

Seems like a good moment to coin an acronym so I don't have to repeat, over and over, the same account of the pieces that make up the problem. How about "Behaviors of Users Modified, and Made into an Empire for Rent"? BUMMER.

BUMMER is a machine, a statistical machine that lives in the computing clouds. To review, phenomena that are statistical and fuzzy are nevertheless real. Even at their best, BUMMER algorithms can only calculate the *chances* that a person will act in a particular way. But what might be only a chance for each person approaches being a certainty *on the average* for large numbers of people. The overall population can be affected with greater predictability than can any single person.

Since BUMMER's influence is statistical, the menace is a little like climate change. You can't say climate change is responsible for a particular storm, flood, or drought, but you can say it changes the odds that they'll happen. In the longer term, the most horrible stuff like sea level rise and the need to relocate most people and find new sources of food would be attributable to climate change, but by then the argument would have been lost.

Similarly, I can't prove that any particular asshole has been made more asshole-y by BUMMER, nor can I prove that any particular degradation of our society would not have happened anyway. There's no certain way to know if BUMMER has changed your behavior, though later on I'll offer some ways to find clues. If you use BUMMER platforms, you've probably been changed at least a little.

While we can't know what details in our world would be different without BUMMER, we can know about the big picture. Like climate change, BUMMER will lead us into hell if we don't self-correct.

THE PARTS THAT MAKE UP THE
BUMMER MACHINE

BUMMER is a machine with six moving parts.

Here's a mnemonic for the six components of the BUM-MER machine, in case you ever have to remember them for a test:

A is for Attention Acquisition leading to Asshole supremacy
B is for Butting into everyone's lives
C is for Cramming content down people's throats
D is for Directing people's behaviors in the sneakiest way possible
E is for Earning money from letting the worst assholes secretly screw with everyone else
F is for Fake mobs and Faker society

Here's a description of each part.

A is for Attention Acquisition leading to Asshole supremacy

People often get weird and nasty online. This bizarre phenomenon surprised everyone in the earliest days of networking, and it has had a profound effect on our world. While not every online experience is nasty, the familiar nastiness colors and bounds the overall online experience. Nastiness also turned out to be like crude oil for the social media companies and other behavior manipulation empires that quickly came to dominate the internet, because it fueled negative behavioral feedback.

Why does the nastiness happen? This will be explored in the next argument. In brief: Ordinary people are brought together in a setting in which the main—or often the only—reward that's available is attention. They can't reasonably expect to earn money, for instance. Ordinary users can gain only fake power and wealth, not real power or wealth. So mind games become dominant.

With nothing else to seek but attention, ordinary people tend to become assholes, because the biggest assholes get the most attention. This inherent bias toward assholedom flavors the action of all the other parts of the BUMMER machine.

B *is for Butting into everyone's lives*

Component B was already introduced in the first argument.

Everyone is placed under a level of surveillance straight out of a dystopian science fiction novel. Pervasive spying could theoretically exist without the asshole-generating platforms in component A, but as it happens, the world we have created connects the two components most of the time.

Spying is accomplished mostly through connected personal devices—especially, for now, smartphones—that people keep practically glued to their bodies. Data are gathered about each person's communications, interests, movements, contact with others, emotional reactions to circumstances, facial expressions, purchases, vital signs: an ever growing, boundless variety of data.

If you're reading this on an electronic device, for instance, there's a good chance an algorithm is keeping a record of data such as how fast you read or when you take a break to check something else.

Algorithms correlate data from each person and between people. The correlations are effectively theories about the nature of each person, and those theories are constantly measured and rated for how predictive they are. Like all well-managed theories, they improve over time through adaptive feedback.

C *is for Cramming content down people's throats*

Algorithms choose what each person experiences through their devices. This component might be called a feed, a recommendation engine, or personalization.

Component C means each person sees different things. The immediate motivation is to deliver stimuli for *individualized* behavior modification.

BUMMER makes it harder to understand why others think and act the way they do. The effects of this component will be examined more in the arguments about how you are losing access to truth and the capacity for empathy.

(Not all personalization is part of BUMMER. When Netflix recommends a movie or eBay recommends something for you to buy, it isn't BUMMER. It only becomes BUMMER in connection with other components. Neither Netflix nor eBay is being paid by third parties to influence your behavior apart from the immediate business you do with each site.)

D *is for Directing people's behaviors in the sneakiest way possible*

The above elements are connected to create a measurement and feedback machine that deliberately modifies behavior. The process was described in the first argument.

To review: Customized feeds become optimized to "engage" each user, often with emotionally potent cues, leading to addiction. People don't realize how they are being manipulated. The default purpose of manipulation is to get people more and more glued in, and to get them to spend more and more time in the system.[7] But other purposes for manipulation are also tested.

---

[7] The television era tried its best to be BUMMER, but without direct feedback loops to individuals. Through heroic effort, television was able to be slightly BUMMER

For instance, if you're reading on a device, your reading behaviors will be correlated with those of multitudes of other people. If someone who has a reading pattern similar to yours bought something after it was pitched in a particular way, then the odds become higher that you will get the same pitch. You might be targeted before an election with weird posts that have proven to bring out the inner cynic in people who are similar to you, in order to reduce the chances that you'll vote.

BUMMER platforms have proudly reported on how they've experimented with making people sad, changing voter turnout, and reinforcing brand loyalty. Indeed, these are some of the best-known examples of research that were revealed in the formative days of BUMMER.[8]

The digital network approach to behavior modification flattens all these examples, all these different slices of life, into one slice. From the point of view of the algorithm, emotions, happiness, and brand loyalty are just different, but similar, signals to optimize.

If it turns out that certain kinds of posts make you sad, and an algorithm is trying to make you sad, then there will be more such posts. No one will necessarily ever know why those particular posts had an effect on you, and you will probably not even notice that a particular post made you a little sad, or that you were being manipulated. The effect is subtle, but cumulative. While scientists sometimes dive in to try to glean insights, for the most part the process takes place in darkness, running on automatic; it's a new kind of sinister shadow cosmos.

The algorithms are rarely interrogated, least of all by external or independent scientists, in part because it's hard to understand why they work. They improve automatically, through feedback,

---

even without much data. "Cultivation theory" studies the phenomenon. See https://en.wikipedia.org/wiki/Cultivation_theory

[8] This history will be recounted in later arguments.

One of the secrets of present-day Silicon Valley is that some people seem to be better than others at getting machine learning schemes to work, and no one understands why. The most mechanistic method of manipulating human behavior turns out to be a surprisingly intuitive art. Those who are good at massaging the latest algorithms become stars and earn spectacular salaries.

E *is for Earning money from letting the worst assholes secretly screw with everyone else*

The mass behavior modification machine is rented out to make money. BUMMER manipulations are not perfect, but they are powerful enough that it becomes suicidal for brands, politicians, and other competitive entities to forgo payments to BUMMER machines. Universal cognitive blackmail ensues, resulting in a rising global spend on BUMMER.[9]

If someone isn't paying a BUMMER platform in cash, then they must turn themselves into data-fuel for that platform in order to not be overwhelmed by it. When Facebook emphasized "news" in its feed, the entire world of journalism had to reformulate itself to BUMMER standards. To avoid being left out, journalists had to create stories that emphasized clickbait and were detachable from context. They were forced to become BUMMER in order to not be annihilated by BUMMER.

BUMMER has not only darkened the ethics of Silicon

---

[9] While digital spending on advertising and marketing might still be a little shy of half of all such spending globally—remember TV is still strong, especially for the aging generations that grew up with it—overall spending is going up, most *new* spending is digital, and almost all of that is BUMMER. Why should a society be spending more and more of its wealth on "advertising"? There are a huge number of industry reports on this topic, and estimates vary, but most analysts agree on this overall interpretation.

Valley; it has made the rest of the economy crazy. The economic side of BUMMER will be explored in Argument Nine.

Before moving on to Component F, I must explain the special role Component E plays in providing the financial incentives that keep the whole BUMMER machine in motion. If you hang out in Silicon Valley, you'll hear a lot of chatter about how money is becoming obsolete, how we're creating forms of power and influence that transcend money. Yet everybody still seems to be chasing money!

If owning everyone's attention by making the world terrifying happens to be what earns the most money, then that is what will happen, even if it means that bad actors are amplified. If we want something different to happen, then the way money is earned has to change.

In the wake of the 2016 elections in the United States, Facebook, Twitter, Google Search, and YouTube[10] announced policy changes to combat dark ads, malicious fake news, hate speech, and so on. Regulators have also introduced requirements such as identifying political advertisers. Just as I was finishing this book, Facebook announced that it will deemphasize news in its feed; the journalism world celebrated, for the most part, because now it might become freer to connect to audiences on its own terms.

---

[10] Why is Google counted as alpha BUMMER? For one thing, Google invented the stuff before Facebook existed. Even so, if you're using only certain Google offerings, like Docs, you might not *experience* Google as BUMMER. Google's search, YouTube, and certain other services meet the criteria for BUMMER, however, even though they're not usually classified as social networking. YouTube uses an adaptive profile of you to drive a personalized feed of videos that is designed to be addictive, including an often nasty comments section, and it makes money when third parties pay to change what you see in order to change your behavior. Classic BUMMER. Furthermore, the content of your seemingly non-BUMMER Google activities, like composing emails, contributes data to the model that drives the BUMMER part.

These changes might very well have a de-BUMMing effect, at least for a while. Indeed, policy tweaks have improved nasty online social phenomena before. Reddit banned some ugly subreddits in 2015, and the flow of hate-posting lessened.

But tweaking doesn't undo the underlying incentives, so bad actors are likely to invent ever sneakier and more sophisticated countermeasures. That has also happened. To state the obvious, there's a rather vast industry called search engine optimization that's devoted to helping clients manipulate the constant policy changes at search engines.

If the incentives remain unchanged, can incremental reforms solve the problems of addiction, manipulation, and worldwide insanity inducement that BUMMER has wrought? If limited reforms can make a difference, I'm all for them, and I hope changes to Facebook's feed make the world a little better, but I fear tweaking cannot achieve enough. That is one of my reasons for writing this book.

Underlying incentives tend to overpower policies. The way that people get around rules in order to chase incentives often makes the world into a darker and more dangerous place. Prohibitions generally don't work. When the United States attempted to outlaw alcohol in the early twentieth century, the result was a rise of organized crime. The ban had to be rescinded. When marijuana was outlawed later in the century, the same thing happened. Prohibitions are engines of corruption that split societies into official and criminal sectors. Laws work best when they are reasonably aligned with incentives.

Tweaking the rules of BUMMER without changing the underlying incentives will probably meet a similar failure. Tweaks have already failed: BUMMER pioneers like Google and Facebook have avidly chased bad actors, fakers, and unsanctioned manipulators, and the result has been the rise of technically accomplished, underground cyber mafias, sometimes working for unfriendly states.

The most dispiriting side effect of BUMMER policy-tweaking is that each cycle in the arms race between platforms and bad actors motivates more and more well-meaning people to demand that BUMMER companies take over more and more of our lives. We ask remote, giant tech companies to govern hate speech, malicious falsified news, bullying, racism, harassment, identity deception, and other nasty things. Well-intentioned activists demand that corporations govern behavior more and more. "Please tell us what we can say, oh rich young programmers of Silicon Valley! Discipline us!" The bad actors who wish to discredit democracy using the BUMMER machine win even when losing ground to well-meaning activists.

There are examples of unfortunate BUMMER incentives throughout this book. Argument Nine proposes a different incentive structure that might make the world better. Onward to Component F!

F *is for Fake mobs and Faker society*

This component is almost always present, even though it typically wasn't part of the initial design of a BUMMER machine. Fake people are present in unknown but vast numbers and establish the ambiance. Bots, AIs, agents, fake reviewers, fake friends, fake followers, fake posters, automated catfishers: a menagerie of wraiths.

Invisible social vandalism ensues. Social pressure, which is so influential in human psychology and behavior, is synthesized.

The crucial role of fake people will be explored in the argument about Truth, which comes after the next one about Assholes.

THE PROBLEM IS LIMITED,
SO WE CAN CONTAIN IT

The more specifically we can draw a line around a problem, the more solvable that problem becomes. Here I have put forward a hypothesis that our problem is not the internet, smartphones, smart speakers, or the art of algorithms. Instead, the problem that has made the world so dark and crazy lately is the BUMMER machine, and the core of the BUMMER machine is not a technology, exactly, but a style of *business plan* that spews out perverse incentives and corrupts people.

It's not even a widely used business plan. Outside of China, the only tech giants that fully depend on BUMMER are Facebook and Google. The other three of the big five tech companies indulge in BUMMER occasionally, because it is normalized these days, but they don't depend on it. A few smaller BUMMER companies are also influential, like Twitter,[11] though they often struggle. One of the reasons I'm optimistic is that BUMMER isn't great as a long-term business strategy. I'll explain that observation more in the argument about economics.

Which companies are BUMMER? This can be debated! A good way to tell is that first-rank BUMMER companies are the ones that attract efforts or spending from bad actors like Russian state intelligence warfare units. This test reveals that there are pseudo-BUMMER services that contain only subsets of the components, like Reddit and 4chan, but still play significant roles in the BUMMER ecosystem.

Next-order services that might become BUMMER but haven't achieved scale are operated by the other tech giants,

---

[11] https://slate.com/technology/2018/03/twitter-is-rethinking-everything-at-last .html

Microsoft, Amazon, and Apple, as well as by smaller companies like Snap.

But this second argument is not about corporations, it's about you. Because we can draw a line around the BUMMER machine, we can draw a line around what to avoid.

The problem with BUMMER is not that it includes any particular technology, but that it's someone else's power trip.

Methodical behaviorism, described in the first argument, isn't in itself a problem, for instance. You might choose to be treated by a cognitive behavioral therapist, and benefit from it. Hopefully that therapist will have sworn an oath to uphold professional standards and will earn your trust. If, however, your therapist is beholden to a giant, remote corporation and is being paid to get you to make certain decisions that aren't necessarily in your own interests, then that would be a BUMMER.

Similarly, hypnotism isn't in itself a BUMMER. But if your hypnotist is replaced by someone you don't know who is working for someone else you don't know, and you have no way of knowing what you're being hypnotized to do, then that *would* be a BUMMER.

The problem isn't any particular technology, but the use of technology to manipulate people, to concentrate power in a way that is so nuts and creepy that it becomes a threat to the survival of civilization.

If you want to help make the world sane, you don't need to give up your smartphone, using computer cloud services, or visiting websites. You don't need to fear math, the social sciences, or psychology.

BUMMER is the stuff to avoid. Delete your BUMMER accounts!

SOCIAL MEDIA IS MAKING YOU INTO AN ASSHOLE

Let me rephrase this argument's title. I don't know you. I'm not saying that you personally are definitely turning into an asshole, but many people are, yet they seem to only see that many *other* people are. I've seen myself start turning into an asshole online, and it was scary and depressing.

So what I should really say is something like "You're vulnerable to gradually turning into an asshole, or statistically you might very well be turning into an asshole. So, no offense, but please take the possibility seriously."

SOOTY SNOW

Addicts can try to hide an addiction, especially from themselves, but often it shows. Personalities change.

The deeply addicted person's rhythm becomes nervous, a compulsive pecking at his situation; he's always deprived, rushing for affirmation. Addicts become anxious, strangely focused on portentous events that aren't visible to others. They are selfish, so wrapped up in their cycle that they don't have much time to notice what others are feeling or thinking about. There's an arrogance, a fetish for exaggeration, that by all appearances is a cover for profound insecurity. A personal mythology overtakes addicts. They see themselves grandiosely and, as they descend further into addiction, ever less realistically.

Hard-core social media addicts display these changes, just like junkies or ruinous gamblers. More commonly, BUMMER users become a *little* like this, statistically more likely to behave like an addict at any given time. There are shades of gray, just as with everything else about BUMMER. The whole society has darkened a few shades as a result.

The most curious feature of the addict's personality is that the addict eventually seems to seek out suffering, since suffering is part of the cycle of scratching the itch. A gambler is addicted not to winning, exactly, but to the process in which losing is more likely. A junkie is addicted not just to the high, but to the vertiginous difference between the lows and the highs.

Similarly, a BUMMER addict eventually becomes preternaturally quick to take offense, as if hoping to get into a spat.

Addicts also become aggressive, though they feel they are acting out of necessity. The choice is to victimize or be a victim. Even successful and pleasant BUMMER addicts, like top social media influencers, have reported that they must not be too nice to others, for that shows weakness[1] in a highly competitive fishbowl. One must be followed more than one follows, for appearances' sake.

The characteristic personality change is hard to perceive or acknowledge in oneself, but easier to see in others, especially if

---

[1] https://www.nytimes.com/2017/12/30/business/hollywood-apartment-social-media.html

you don't like them. When conservative BUMMER addicts dislike liberal college students with BUMMER addictions, they sometimes use the insult "poor little snowflake."

The poorest snowflake of them all, however, is Donald Trump, who exhibits the same behavior. I met him a few times over several decades, and I didn't like him, but he wasn't a BUMMER addict back then. He was a New York City character, a manipulator, an actor, a master at working the calculus of chums and outcasts. But as a character he was in on his own joke. Even reality TV didn't really make him lose it.

As a Twitter addict, Trump has changed. He displays the snowflake pattern and sometimes loses control. He is not acting like the most powerful person in the world, because his addiction is more powerful. Whatever else he might be, whatever kind of victimizer, he is also a victim.

MEETING MY INNER TROLL

Many things about social media have changed over the years, but the basic form was already around when I first got into computers in the late 1970s. The social media we had back then amounted to little more than commenting, just a bunch of people adding their text. There wasn't any voting for favorite posts, nor did algorithms customize your feed. Very basic.

But I noticed something horrifying all those years ago. Sometimes, out of nowhere, I would get into a fight with someone, or a group of people. It was so weird. We'd start insulting each other, trying to score points, getting under each other's skin. And about incredibly stupid stuff, like whether or not someone knew what they were talking about when it came to brands of pianos. Really.

I'd stew between posts. "I am *not* ignorant! I know about pianos! How dare that moron say those horrible things about me? I know, I'll ruin his reputation by tricking him into saying something stupid."

This happened so often that it became normal. Not just for me, but for everyone. It was chaotic human weather. There'd be a nice morning and suddenly a storm would roll in.

In order to avoid falling into asshole behavior you had to make yourself fake-nice. You'd have to be saccharine polite, constantly choosing your words super carefully, walking on eggshells.

That sucked worse!

I just stopped using the stuff because I didn't like who I was becoming. You know the adage that you should choose a partner on the basis of who you become when you're around the person? That's a good way to choose technologies, too.

When some friends started a pioneering online community called the Well in the 1990s, they gave me an account, but I never posted a single thing. Same story much later, when I helped some buddies start an online world called Second Life.

In the early 2000s, an enterprising woman named Arianna Huffington got me to blog on her Huffington Post for a while. I have to tell you how she did it.

We were at a fancy conference for rich and influential people at a fancy little town in the Colorado Rockies. I was sitting on a bench with my arm resting on the rim of a rounded cement wall surrounding a garbage can. Arianna came along and sat on my arm, trapping it. "Arianna—oh, you didn't notice; let me get my arm out."

In her thick Greek accent: "Do you know what some men would pay for this privilege? I will release your hand if you will blog for me."

So I did it. Briefly I was one of the HuffPost's top bloggers, always on the front page. But I found myself falling into that old problem again whenever I read the comments, and I could not get myself to ignore them. I would feel this weird low-level boiling rage inside me. Or I'd feel this absurd glow when people liked what I wrote, even if what they said didn't indicate that they had paid much attention to it. Comment authors were mostly seeking attention for themselves.

We were all in the same stew, manipulating each other, inflating ourselves.

After a short while, I noticed that I'd write things I didn't even believe in order to get a rise out of readers. I wrote stuff that I knew people wanted to hear, or the opposite, because I knew it would be inflammatory.

Oh my God! I was back in that same place, becoming an asshole because of *something* about this stupid technology!

I quit—again.

Of all the ten arguments in this book, this is the one that really gets to me viscerally. I don't want to be an asshole. Or a fake-nice person.

I want to be authentically nice, and certain online designs seem to fight against that with magical force. That's the core reason why I don't have accounts on Facebook, Twitter, WhatsApp,[2] Instagram, Snapchat, or any of the rest. You'll see fake accounts in my name. There's even a supposed @RealJaronLanier on Twitter. But I have no idea who that is. Not me.

I don't think I'm better than you because I don't have social media accounts. Maybe I'm worse; maybe you can handle the stuff better than I can.

---

[2] WhatsApp is part of Facebook; even if it sometimes feels like any other texting platform, it's in fact a primary data scooper for BUMMER. Facebook has faced considerable legal blowback for using WhatsApp data that way in Europe (see https://www.theverge.com/2017/12/18/16792448/whatsapp-facebook-data -sharing-no-user-consent). In the United States, since the network neutrality rules are being relaxed, it's possible that *all* texting, even native texting between phones, will become part of BUMMER, but as of this writing it doesn't appear to have happened.

But I've observed that since social media took off, assholes are having more of a say in the world.

BUMMER platform experiences ricochet between two extremes. Either there's a total shitstorm of assholes (that's not a mixed metaphor, right?) or everyone is super careful and artificially nice.

The biggest assholes get the most attention, however, and they often end up giving a platform its flavor. Even if there are corners of the platform where not everyone is an asshole all the time, those corners feel penned in, because the assholes are waiting just outside. It's part of how BUMMER Component A pushes tribalism.

THE MYSTERIOUS NATURE OF ASSHOLE AMPLIFICATION TECHNOLOGY

No one has convinced me that they have a complete understanding of why Component A brings out one's inner asshole. There are many theories,[3] but here are the ideas that have served me best.

It's not helpful to think of the world as being divided into assholes and non-assholes, or if you prefer, trolls and victims.

Each of us has an inner troll. In the early days, before everyone was doing it, the air was clearer and it was easier to notice how bizarre it is when your inner troll starts talking. It's like an ugly alien living inside you that you long ago forgot about. Don't let your inner troll take control! If it happens when you're in a particular situation, avoid that situation! It

---

[3] The most prominent current academic approach to the study of asshole creation is SIDE Theory. See https://en.wikipedia.org/wiki/Social_identity_model_of_deindividuation _effects, but please promise me you won't become a jerk in an edit war about this entry, okay? If you want to read relevant research from a scientist working for Facebook, see the work of Justin Cheng: https://www.clr3.com/.

doesn't matter if it's an online platform, a relationship, or a job. Your character is like your health, more valuable than anything you can buy. Don't throw it away.

But why, *why* is the inner troll there at all?

It's such a common problem that it must be a deep, primal business, a tragedy of our inheritance, a stupid flaw at the heart of the human condition. But saying that doesn't get us anywhere. What exactly *is* the inner troll?

Sometimes the inner troll takes charge, sometimes it doesn't. My working hypothesis has long been that there's a switch deep in every human personality that can be set in one of two modes. We're like wolves. We can either be solitary or members of a pack of wolves. I call this switch the Solitary/Pack switch.

When we're solitary wolves, we're more free. We're cautious, but also capable of more joy. We think for ourselves, improvise, create. We scavenge, hunt, hide. We howl once in a while out of pure exuberance.

When we're in a pack, interactions with others become the most important thing in the world. I don't know how far that goes with wolves, but it's dramatic in people. When people are locked in a competitive, hierarchical power structure, as in a corporation, they can lose sight of the reality of what they're doing because the immediate power struggle looms larger than reality itself.

The example that looms largest today is climate change denialism. In the scientific community and among virtually all nations in the world, there's a consensus that we must confront it, and yet a small but powerful group of businesspeople and politicians don't buy it. They perceive the science of climate change as a plot to attack their wealth and power. That's an absurd notion, an absurdity that's only possible when you're locked into understanding the world solely in terms of human power struggles, to the exclusion of the larger reality.

For a creature of the technical world, it's comforting to highlight an example like that, because it lets us off the hook, but scientific communities can also suffer from the switch being set to Pack. For instance, the theoretical physicist Lee Smolin documented how string theorists exerted mob rule for a while in the world of theoretical physics.[4] The pattern is found whenever people form into groups. Street gangs perceive only pack concepts such as territory and revenge, even as they destroy their lives, families, and neighborhoods. The Pack setting of the switch makes you pay so much attention to your peers and enemies in the world of packs that you can become blind to what's happening right in front of your face.

When the Solitary/Pack switch is set to Pack, we become obsessed with and controlled by a pecking order. We pounce on those below us, lest we be demoted, and we do our best to flatter and snipe at those above us at the same time. Our peers flicker between "ally" and "enemy" so quickly that we cease to perceive them as individuals. They become archetypes from a comic book. The only constant basis of friendship is shared antagonism toward other packs.

Yes, I'm mixing animal metaphors. Sure, I think a modern "domesticated" cat is more like a solitary wolf than like a wolf in a pack, though cats are also intensely concerned with hierarchical social structures. Maybe cats have a Pride switch, and living with people gave them the freedom to deemphasize prides. The richer the hunting ground, the easier it is to not be an asshole toward your peers. Moving in with people might have been for cats what advancing technology has been for people. More options means more chances to not be a troll. At least that's what advancing technology has usually meant in the big

---

[4] http://leesmolin.com/writings/the-trouble-with-physics/

picture of human history. BUMMER is an unfortunate exception, a way of using technology to reduce human freedom.

The switch in people should generally be kept in the Solitary Wolf position.

When people are solitary wolves, then each individual has access to slightly different information about the world, and slightly different ways of thinking about that information. I've been talking about the relationship between the Solitary setting and personal character, but there are other reasons to keep the switch in the Solitary position.

Consider a demonstration that is often enacted on the first day of business school. A professor shows a class a big jar of jelly beans and asks each person to estimate the number of beans. Averaging all the estimates usually results in a pretty accurate count. Each person brings different perspectives, cognitive styles, skills, and strategies to the mystery, and the average gets at the agreements between them. (This only works for single-number answers. If you ask a committee to design a product or write a novel, the result comes out like something made by a committee.)

Now suppose that the students could look at the jar only through photos in a social media feed. Different camps of people with different ideas about the number of beans would form and would ridicule each other. Russian intelligence services would add pictures of similar jars with different numbers of beans. Bean promoters would motivate trolls to argue that there aren't enough beans and you must buy more. And so on. There would no longer be a way to guess the number of beans because the power of diversity will have been compromised. When that happens, markets can no longer offer utility to the world.

You can replace the jar with a political candidate, a product, or anything else. But that brings up problems that I'll tackle in the arguments about how BUMMER ruins our access to truth and meaning.

For now, think of the jar in this example as being like your identity, as it is presented through social media. Your identity is Packified by BUMMER. By putting yourself out there, you are erasing yourself. As long as people are thinking for themselves, then collectively they'll guess the number of jelly beans in the jar, but that won't work if they're in a pack and stuck in groupthink.

There are situations that call for the switch to be set to Pack. Military units are the canonical example. Sometimes people must lose themselves to a hierarchical order because that's the only way to survive. But a primary goal of civilization should be to make those times as rare as possible.

Capitalism fails when the switch is set to Pack. The Pack setting causes market bubbles and other market failures. There are certainly noisy businesspeople who prefer military metaphors for business; you're supposed to be tough and ruthless. But since the Pack setting also makes you partially blind, in the long run that personality style is not great for business, if we define business as being about reality beyond social competitions.

When people act as solitary wolves, then each person is in a unique position in society and thinks in a unique way. Another example: Democratic elections are a genuine commingling of ideas, and have historically helped societies find paths forward despite controversy, but only so long as people are switched to Solitary. Democracy fails when the switch is set to Pack. Tribal voting, personality cults, and authoritarianism are the politics of the Pack setting.

It might sound like a contradiction at first, but it isn't; collective processes make the best sense when participants are acting as individuals.

THE MOST MASTERFUL MASTER SWITCH[5]

Suppose you believe the theory of the Solitary/Pack switch. What is it about online experiences that turns the switch to the Pack setting? The simplest answer is probably the right one. The switch will turn to the Pack setting when the benefits of the Solitary Wolf setting are made obscure.

When you are a solitary wolf, you are forced to get directly in touch with the larger reality that doesn't care about what a society thinks. You must find water and shelter, or you will perish. You have to scavenge and hunt for yourself. Your personality shifts; you must solve problems on the basis of evidence you gather on your own, instead of by paying attention to group perception. You take on the qualities of a scientist or an artist.

When you're in a pack, social status and intrigues become more immediate than the larger reality. You become more like an operator, a politician, or a slave.

Therefore, situations in which you are separated from immediate contact with larger reality, in which social interactions become preeminent, will turn your inner switch to Pack.

Aside from ringing true, this theory matches available evidence. For instance, of the large social networks, the one with the fewest assholes is LinkedIn.[6] That doesn't mean that LinkedIn doesn't have other BUMMER problems. Tristan Harris singles it out for criticism related to exploiting social anxieties in the name of engagement, for example.[7]

Full disclosure: I have a professional connection to LinkedIn that might impair my objectivity (even though I don't have an

---

[5] Shout-out to Tim Wu.

[6] https://www.recode.net/2016/12/29/14100064/linkedin-daniel-roth-fake-news
-facebook-recode-podcast

[7] http://www.spiegel.de/international/zeitgeist/smartphone-addiction-is-part-of-the
-design-a-1104237.html

account on the site). You should not accept what I say without thinking about it critically, and my disclosure of a conflict of interest is a great starting point to do that. Think for yourself!

Anyway, while the people I know at LinkedIn are lovely, I can also say that about people I know at Twitter and Facebook. The difference with LinkedIn is simply that users of LinkedIn have *something* to do other than compete for social appearances—something with meatier stakes. The site is well known as a place to further your career. It makes money mostly by connecting employers with hires rather than by manipulating people to make purchases or change their behavior in other off-topic ways.

Careers are physical, real processes that generate sustenance. They are not only real but also nonfungible. Each career is both unique and indispensable to a person. LinkedIn users aren't all seeking exactly the same career, so they aren't forced precisely into direct conflict or politics with one another. They aren't each assigned a popularity number, like social media aspirants who are thrust into a single global competition.

Users on LinkedIn have something to do other than social posing, which tends to fuel assholes; and most people will choose to be something other than an asshole, *given the choice*. A prevalent layer of motivation to do *anything* aside from attention-getting or seeking other purely psychological rewards is the key. That simple quality, that there are stakes beyond mind games, elevates an online environment.

It's that simple. Practicality—which includes how you make a living—is ultimately what unites, and therefore civilizes us.[8]

---

[8] When you're not on BUMMER it becomes possible to be tough and yet not a jerk. What I hope is happening in this book is that I'm using salty language and getting emotional, and yet I don't vilify and condemn people. "BUMMER sucks, but it's mostly just a stupid business plan, and the people behind it are usually great and just made a mistake and we all need to outgrow it." See? It's not that hard to be firm and intense without having to hate. In fact, out here in reality, it's hard to even remember

In BUMMERland, it seems as if every little comment either turns into a contest for total personal invalidation and destruction, or else everyone has to get all nicey-nicey and fake. The obvious example is that the BUMMER-addicted U.S. president, the social media addict–in—chief, turns everything into a contest over who can destroy someone else most completely with a tweet, or else who gets good treatment in exchange for total loyalty.

GO TO WHERE YOU ARE KINDEST

Of course there were assholes in the world before BUMMER, but it wasn't as hard to avoid being one. On BUMMER you have to fight gravity just to be decent.

The online asshole-supremacy problem could be solved rather easily simply by dumping the BUMMER model of business. One possibility is that people could earn money more often and more fairly from what they do online; that idea will be explored in the argument about how social media is ruining economics.

What we need is *anything* that's real beyond social pretensions that people can focus on instead of becoming assholes.

In the meantime, there is something you can do personally. If, when you participate in online platforms, you notice a nasty thing inside yourself, an insecurity, a sense of low self-esteem, a yearning to lash out, to swat someone down, *then leave that platform*. Simple.

There is a spotlight on online bullying, as there should be, and you might have experienced being bullied online. Many, many people have.

---

what it feels like to have your inner troll try to take over. That's why I'm writing this as a book instead of an online post.

But I am also asking you to notice, within your own mind, in genuine secrecy—don't share this—if you are feeling the temptation to strike out at *someone else* online. Maybe that other person started it. Whatever. It isn't worth it. Leave the platform. Don't post that insult video, don't tweet in retaliation.

If Twitter ceased operations tomorrow, not only would Trump not be able to tweet, obviously, but also I believe he'd become a nicer, better person at all hours, at least until he latched on to another BUMMER platform.

I can't prove this, and a lot of people will disagree with me. That doesn't matter. Look into yourself. Seriously, are you being as kind as you want to be? At what times are you more like the person you want to be, and when do you get irritable or dismissive?

Your character is the most precious thing about you. Don't let it degrade.

SOCIAL MEDIA IS
UNDERMINING TRUTH

EVERYBODY KNOWS

The notion that truth has recently become dead is one of the most familiar tropes of our times.[1] And the murderer most often accused is social media, or a certain president who is addicted to social media. Articles with titles like "How Technology Disrupted the Truth"[2] are plentiful enough that I hardly need to pile on.

This book contains varied explanations for how and why social media undermines truth; the explanations are central to each of the other nine arguments.

Furthermore, each of components A–F of BUMMER destroys truth in its own way.

---

[1] https://backissues.time.com/storefront/2017/is-truth-dead-/prodTD20170403
.html

[2] https://www.theguardian.com/media/2016/jul/12/how-technology-disrupted-the
-truth

A Assholes change discourse into discharge. They turn the Solitary/Pack switch to Pack, which makes people pay so much attention to social status competition that they can become blinded to everything else, to any broader or more fundamental truth.

B Tech companies spy on you, Butting into your life. The perception of truth requires that people be authentic, so that they can perceive authentically. This principle was explained in the analogy of the jelly beans in the jar. When people are constantly prodded by spying technologies, they lose authenticity.

C Cramming experiences down your throat. When what people can be made to perceive *is* the product sold by some of the richest corporations, then obviously truth must suffer. The loss of truth is the product.

D Directing lives through ubiquitous behavior modification. When engineered addictions are applied to manipulate masses of people for commercial gain, obviously those masses become removed from truth. That is precisely the point.

E Earning money by letting some people, often nasty ones, secretly modify the behaviors of other people. Economic incentives tend to win over rules, policies, and good intentions, as will be explained in the Argument to come about economics. Therefore, incentives in BUMMER often disfavor truth. At best, they aren't aligned with truth.

F Fake people have no reason to tell the truth. Indeed, truth is suicide to a fake person. But fake people have been bred and amplified by BUMMER.

Truth, meaning a claim that can be tested or events that are honestly documented—the stuff that *all* people can hold in common—is by definition anathema to the manipulations of BUMMER. BUMMER must often route around truth and attempt to suppress it in order to thrive.

WHEN PEOPLE ARE FAKE, EVERYTHING BECOMES FAKE

The fake people from Component F are stem cells for all the other fakeness in BUMMER.

Leaving aside explicitly fake people like Alexa, Cortana, and Siri, you might think that you've never interacted with a fake person online, but you have, and with loads of them. You decided to buy something because it had a lot of good reviews, but many of those reviews were from artificial people. You found a doctor by using a search engine, but the reason that doctor showed up high in the search results was that a load of fake people linked to her office. You looked at a video or read a story because so many other people had, but most of them were fake. You became aware of tweets because they were retweeted first by armies of bots.

Our peer groups influence us profoundly when we're young, but that remains true throughout life. If your extended peer group contains a lot of fake people, calculated to manipulate you, you are likely to be influenced without even realizing it.

This is a difficult truth to accept, but because of the importance of social perception, it is true to at least a small degree that you have been living a fake life yourself. BUMMER is making *you* partially fake.

Whatever you can do, bots can do a million times while you blink. Fake people are a *cultural* denial-of-service attack.

In a denial-of-service attack, hackers get a bot army to bombard a site with so much traffic that no real person can access it. This is a typical way that bad actors make use of computer viruses. They infect millions of computers with a virus and then get those computers to contact a victim site all at once. Or, more commonly, they sell that ability as a service.

In the same way, armies of fake people on a BUMMER platform take up a lot of the oxygen in the room and steer the world on behalf of their masters.

Fake people are typically not operated by the same people who operate BUMMER platforms; instead, fake people are manufactured in a new underworld. There is now an industry that sells counterfeit humans.

According to reporting by the *New York Times*, the going rate for fake people on Twitter in early 2018 was $225 for the first 25,000 fake followers.[3] The fake accounts might be mash-ups of accounts from real people; on casual inspection, they seem real. Celebrities, businesses, politicians, and a more modern pool of cyber-bad-actor customers all make use of fake-people factories. The companies that sell fake people are often fake as well. (The *Times* found that one prominent bot service listed a fake address.)

Some sites might not even exist were it not for fake people. The best-known example might be Ashley Madison, a purported introduction service for adulterers. The site has reportedly used fake women to lure men into signing up for more expensive accounts.[4] It has even been accused of creating fake critics to drum up controversy to promote itself.[5]

The mainstream BUMMER companies don't have completely clean hands when it comes to bots. It is hard for main-

[3] https://www.nytimes.com/interactive/2018/01/27/technology/social-media-bots .html

[4] https://www.reuters.com/article/us-ashleymadison-cyber/infidelity-website-ashley -madison-facing-ftc-probe-ceo-apologizes-idUSKCN0ZL09J

[5] https://www.forbes.com/sites/kashmirhill/2011/02/11/ashley-madison-lessons-in -promoting-a-sleazy-business/

stream BUMMER operators to get rid of fake people entirely, because they become codependent, in the way that animals need gut bacteria. Component F provides momentum and free energy. The interlopers become part of the machine.

The tech companies all do battle with fake accounts, but they also benefit from them. While people who work at Twitter might, on an emotional or ethical level, prefer that their platform was bot-free, the bots also amplify the activity and intensity of the service. Massive fake social activities turn out to influence real people. They indirectly create a genuine social reality, which means they make money. People are successfully manipulated by them. Techies might rationalize the situation for themselves, coming up with arguments about how bots increase the diversity of free speech, or some similar nonsense,[6] even though bots can drown out authentic speech.

Another phenomenon that relates to Component F is the way some legacy media outlets, such as Fox News in the USA, have become more cranky and partisan. ("Legacy media" means TV, radio, and print in Silicon Valley-speak.) Why is this happening so overwhelmingly in the social media era when it was more muted before, at least in modern times? There are many reasons to explore, but one reason is surely that BUMMER can be used to craft a social ambience that makes what was once unthinkable thinkable. For example, the craziest conspiracy theories often start on BUMMER, amplified by artificial people, before they appear in hyper-partisan legacy media.[7]

Hyperpartisan outlets like Fox News can therefore be thought of as part of Component F. They are chunks of legacy

---

[6] https://slate.com/technology/2018/01/robots-deserve-a-first-amendment-right-to
-free-speech.html

[7] http://money.cnn.com/2017/05/24/media/seth-rich-fox-news-retraction/index
.html

media that have been jury-rigged to become part of the BUM-
MER machine.[8]

Component F makes the BUMMER machine robust in its
awfulness, so that tweaks attempting to improve it do little
good. For instance, in the United States, regulators have asked
social media companies to begin identifying who paid for an
ad, but since there are uncountable multitudes of fake entities
energizing the BUMMER machine, how can anyone know
what such an identification will mean?

Bots route around attempts to tweak or regulate BUMMER.
If BUMMER ads were to become tightly regulated, for instance,
bots might whip up a blizzard of shitposts[9] to accomplish what
could no longer be done with ads. This is one of the reasons
that BUMMER must be removed from our world.

In testimony before the U.S. Senate, lawyers for social media
companies stated that they couldn't detect the fake people.[10]
They have no means.

This is dark comedy. The BUMMER algorithms are presumably trying to manipulate the fake people, just as they manipulate you; but unlike you, bots are immune.

I must emphasize that the kind of fake person I'm ridiculing
is a mass-produced fraud intended to manipulate. It is absolutely
not my place to judge what is authentic for you or how you
construct your online persona. I'm criticizing a power relationship, not proposing a theory of authenticity. When a teenager

---

[8] That is not to say that there is a conspiracy between new- and old-media companies.
There has been more tension than cooperation. Remember, BUMMER is an automatic system that has been set in motion to optimize itself. It finds patterns that
work, even when those patterns defy the emotional or political tendencies of those
who make money from the patterns. Tensions between Fox News and Facebook are
well known: Facebook is absorbing money that once would have been destined for
old media.

[9] https://www.dailydot.com/unclick/shitposting/

[10] https://www.theguardian.com/us-news/2017/oct/31/facebook-russia-ads-senate
-hearing-al-franken

fakes an Instagram account, that's not necessarily a bad thing. Becoming literate in the ways of one's society is essential if one is to become a first-class citizen in it; if the society is based on fake people, you'd better learn how to make a fake person yourself.

BUMMER KILLS

Much of the damage done by BUMMER can be undone by deleting your accounts, but the social loss of truth spills out from BUMMER and hurts even people who are not engaged directly with BUMMER at all. There are many examples of this danger, especially in politics, but I'll focus here on public health.

I'm a father, and I want the children my daughter interacts with to be immunized. Immunization is a common good, a gift we can give each other. It is one of the greatest inventions in human history.

When I was growing up, there were still plenty of people twisting their way along on sidewalks, suffering from the deformations of polio. The victims who still lived and could walk at all were the lucky ones. It didn't matter if you were rich or poor, black or white. Anyone could get polio.

When was the last time you saw a polio victim? And polio is far from the only example. My parents' generation lived through epidemics that killed millions—tens of millions—of people.

Immunizations are better than electricity, flush toilets, and space exploration all put together. And I really love all those inventions.

But I know other parents—educated, upper-middle-class American parents—who won't even consider vaccinating their kids. Some of them are "left" and some "right." It's not just that they think immunization is bad; they believe that it's evil, alien, and icky. They think it causes autism. They can't get conspiracy theories out of their heads. You might think I'm being elitist when I am more appalled that "educated" parents, who are more likely to be affluent, foment dangerous nonsense, but isn't the whole point of education supposed to be that it diminishes people's susceptibility to dangerous nonsense?

I have tried to engage with these parents, and that's when they show me their BUMMER feeds. Every day they digest memes, fake scare stories, and clickbait that appear to come from bots,[11] though no one really knows to what degree.[12] An ambience of paranoia and dismissal has overtaken these BUMMER addicts as they seek a new fix from positive and negative social stimuli every day.

There have always been weird waves of untruth in society, but somehow, in order to progress into our comfortable modernity, we gradually found a way to truth, together. What is different in recent years is that many of us no longer directly interrogate the jar of jelly beans.

In our BUMMER era, the information reaching people is the result of how manipulative advertisers and power-mad tech companies intersect with crazed, engineered status competitions. That means there's less authenticity in the social exploration that helps us find truth.

People are clustered into paranoia peer groups because then they can be more easily and predictably swayed. The clustering is automatic, sterile, and, as always, weirdly innocent. There wasn't anyone sitting in a tech company who decided to promote anti-vaccine rhetoric as a tactic. It could just as easily have

---

[11] https://respectfulinsolence.com/2017/09/28/antivaxers-on-twitter-fake-news-and-twitter-bots/

[12] https://www.forbes.com/sites/robertglatter/2017/12/23/bot-or-not-how-fake-social-media-accounts-can-jeopardize-your-health/

been anti-hamster rhetoric. The only reason BUMMER reinforces the stuff is that paranoia turns out, as a matter of course, to be an efficient way of corralling attention.

The ability of humans to enjoy our modern luxuries, such as a diminution of deadly epidemics, while even temporarily rejecting the benefits of hard-won truths is a testament to how far we've come as a technological species. Some of us can briefly get away with assuming that people will be healthy without vaccinations, as if health were the natural state of affairs.

Public health measures and modern medicine have doubled our life spans. Doubled! The unintended result is that now some of us can believe nonsense and not pay for that belief with our lives. At least for a while.

In order to benefit in the long term as technology improves, we have to find a way to not let our improved comfort and security turn into cover for a lazy drift into perilous fantasy. Media forms that promote truth are essential for survival, but the dominant media of our age do no such thing.

I focused on this example because it upsets me as a parent; that's a deep level on which to be upset. It's maddening to drive through Silicon Valley and realize that many of my friends working behind all those green glass windows in the low-slung tech company buildings that reach to the horizon might be contributing to a process that's reviving once-defeated diseases in children.[13]

Save children; delete your accounts.

---

[13] https://www.usatoday.com/story/news/nation/2014/04/06/anti-vaccine-movement -is-giving-diseases-a-2nd-life/7007955/

SOCIAL MEDIA IS MAKING
WHAT YOU SAY
MEANINGLESS

What you say isn't meaningful without context.

It's easy to miss this simple fact in our day-to-day, face-to-face lives, because the context is usually obvious. Suppose I say, "Get off me! I can't give you more attention now!" Sounds weird or cruel, unless you see me saying that to our cat Loof (called that because she isn't aloof), who makes genuinely unreasonable demands for attention.

The principle becomes clearer in extreme situations. If you see someone in a car that has fire coming out from under the hood, and you yell "Fire!" then you might save that person's life. If you yell the same thing in a crowded club, you might get people killed in a stampede, whether or not there really is a fire.

Online, we often have little or no ability to know or influence the context in which our expression will be understood. The easiest way to understand the principle is to note extreme examples.

The *best documented* "extreme" examples are the ones where

those doing the expressing have some clout and are able to force a change. For instance, consider this problem for You-Tube advertisers: For a while, it wasn't uncommon for an ad for something innocuous, like soap, to be streamed in sequence with a horrible terrorist-recruitment video. When advertisers complained—and only then, after the fact—Google started to root out terrorist content.[1] Actual money was paid to affected advertisers in compensation. The advertisers are the true customers, so they have a voice. Do ordinary users get to say as much about the context in which they are placed by BUM-MER schemes?

The *most common* extreme examples, however, might arise when women and girls who attempt to express themselves online find that their words and images are sexualized or incorporated into a violent or manipulative framework. Women's online presences have often been grotesquely transformed for the purposes of humiliation, shame, and harassment.[2] Prominent women have faced harassment for years—for example, the women affected by "Gamergate"—but now it's happening to ordinary young women.[3]

These extreme examples occur only because the rules of the game in BUMMER are that you don't know the context in which you are expressing anything and you have no reliable way of knowing how it will be presented to someone else.

This problem has become so pervasive that it's almost invisible, like air. We have given up our connection to context. Social media mashes up meaning. Whatever you say will be contextualized and given meaning by the way algorithms, crowds, and

---

[1] http://www.telegraph.co.uk/technology/2017/07/03/youtube-refunds-advertisers-terror-content-scandal/

[2] https://www.theverge.com/2015/2/4/7982099/twitter-ceo-sent-memo-taking-personal-responsibility-for-the/

[3] http://www.bbc.com/news/uk-england-41693437

crowds of fake people who are actually algorithms mash it up with what other people say.

No one ever knows exactly how what they're saying will be received, but in non-BUMMER situations you usually have reasonable guesses. I speak in public sometimes, and I instinctively adjust my presentation to an audience. I say different things to high school students than I do to a room full of quants.[4] This is just a normal part of communication.

Speaking through social media isn't really speaking at all. Context is applied to what you say after you say it, for someone else's purposes and profit.

This changes what can be expressed. When context is surrendered to the platform, communication and culture become petty, shallow, and predictable. You have to become crazy extreme if you want to say something that will survive even briefly in an unpredictable context. Only asshole communication can achieve that.

MEANING AJAR

BUMMER replaces your context with its context. From the point of view of the algorithms, you are no longer a name, but a number: the number of followers, likes, clicks, or other measures of how much you contributed to the BUMMER machine, moment to moment.

Dystopian science fiction often imagines an evil empire that replaces names with numbers. Real-life prisons do it to prisoners. There's a reason. To become a number is to be explicitly subservient to a system. A number is a public verification of reduced freedom, status, and personhood. It's especially chilling to me, because my mother survived a concentration camp,

---

[4] Mathematicians who work in finance.

where your number was tattooed on your arm. That would be too expensive to do today. The Nazis would just store your number, along with your biometrics, in the cloud.

This might all sound a little too dark to people playing the social media numbers game. I am presented with a thoroughly modern dilemma. If people *want* to be subsumed, then who am I to say, "You should fight for your individual dignity?" Doesn't that make me the one who isn't respecting the wishes of others?

Because of the dilemma I just mentioned, I don't want to criticize people who seem to like the situation—for instance, young people who are trying to be social media influencers. Instead I'll focus on people who are trying to do something other than be a number, even as they are subsumed by the new reality of number supremacy.

Sources of content, such as news websites, are discovered by people mostly through BUMMER, so such sites must game themselves to be favored by algorithms and crowds.

One newsroom I visited recently had big screens up all over the place, similar to a NASA control room, but showing up-to-the-second statistics about each post created by someone in the room. Presumably the writers and other creators are supposed to be glued to these numbers in order to maximize "engagement." They are forced to become components of the BUMMER machine. I feel sorry for them.

This problem has lately been associated with the Facebook feed, but it is a BUMMER-wide failure. It was already a problem before the Facebook feed existed.[5] Now that Facebook has announced it will deemphasize news in its feed, maybe things will get a little better; nonetheless, it's hard to imagine that news will now be instantly free of BUMMER-driven context

---

[5] I wrote about it in my 2010 book *You Are Not a Gadget*.

collapse. In order for the news to regain context, people will have to discover news through non-BUMMER systems. What will these systems be? Hopefully people will develop direct relationships, even more hopefully with subscriptions, to sources of news and other content.

In the meantime, there are many problems with the subsuming of journalism to the god of statistics. Some of the criticisms are familiar: too much clickbait lowers the level of public discourse; writers aren't given the space to take risks.

Remember how BUMMER algorithms are constantly self-optimizing? Except that they fall into ruts? The process was described back in the first argument. Everyone, including journalists, is forced to play the optimization game in hopes of getting the most out of BUMMER. A news source will keep tweaking what it does until further tweaks no longer yield better results. After that, repetition. That's why so much clickbait is so similar. There's only this one weird trick to optimize clickbait.[6]

It's not the tweaking but the BUMMER environment that gets people stuck. Out in the real world, outside of BUMMER, there is enough complexity and subtlety that tweaking doesn't drive everyone to the same stuck place. Feedback is a good thing, but overemphasizing immediate feedback within an artificially limited online environment leads to ridiculous outcomes.[7]

Here's a non-geeky framing of the same idea: What if listening to an inner voice or heeding a passion for ethics or

---

[6] http://www.slate.com/articles/business/moneybox/2013/07/how_one_weird_trick
_conquered_the_internet_what_happens_when_you_click_on.html

[7] Recall the footnote about energy landscapes from the first argument? If you do, then read this footnote! Tweaking to optimize your design within a system that isn't based on the unbounded nature of nature, but is instead based on a bounded, abstract, human construction, will inevitably kill creativity and progress by rutting you in a petty valley in the energy landscape.

beauty were to lead to more important work in the long term, even if it measured as less successful in the moment? What if deeply reaching a small number of people matters more than reaching everybody with nothing?

Some other questions need to be asked. First, why believe the numbers? As discussed in the previous argument, much of the online world is fake. Fake readers, fake commenters, fake referrals. I note that news sites that are trying to woo advertisers directly often seem to show *spectacularly* greater numbers of readers for articles about products that might be advertised— like choosing your next gaming machine—than for articles about other topics.

This doesn't mean the site is fudging its numbers. Instead, a manager probably hired a consulting firm that used an algorithm to optimize the choice of metrics services to relate the kind of usage statistics the site could use to attract advertisers. In other words, the site's owners didn't consciously fudge, but they kinda-sorta know that their stats are part of a giant fudge cake.

Don't blame the site. There are so few independent news sites, and they're precious. They've been backed into a corner by BUMMER and they're incredibly vulnerable. News organizations—especially those supporting expensive investigative journalism—have been told for twenty years that it's up to them to be nimble enough to come up with new business plans that will stand up to the "disruptions" of the big tech companies, but no one has ever come up with actual good advice.

So the news has thinned, even as the news is ever more in the news. There is constant BUMMER obsession with the news, and yet there are almost no investigative local news organizations left in the United States. Our huge nation is only a few organizations away from having no independent newsrooms with resources and clout.

When writers become less motivated by the desire to reach people directly, but instead must appeal to a not necessarily reliable number-dispensing system, then writers are losing their connection to their context. The more successful a writer is in this system, the less she knows what she's writing.

Even when the readers are real, not fake, algorithms are routing them to particular content, so their choices aren't really independent. The measurements aren't valid, by definition. You can't tell someone where to go and then claim that you discovered something new because you learned where that person went. This is yet another ubiquitous problem that's as hard to see as air.

Here's some positive spin: The fact that independent journalism is in trouble in BUMMER's shadow is a sign of its integrity. Journalists have successfully held themselves to higher standards than social media influencers, but they have also paid a price. Now the real news is called "fake news," because by the standards of BUMMER, what is real *is* fake; in BUMMER, reality has been replaced by stupid numbers.

POD PEOPLE

Another way to illuminate the tricky degradation of context is to notice online situations in which it is *not* a problem, at least not yet. A part of the online world that hasn't destroyed its own context—at least as I write, in 2018—is podcasting. It isn't BUMMER yet.

Podcasters are real people, known to the listener. Podcasts are episodic, so they build a sense of personality and context. The listener can't—as yet—jump around audio content as easily as she or he can jump around content that's presented visually, like a website or a video. So a listener's actual experience is more like the experience the podcaster imagines it will be than like what happens when someone uses a BUMMER feed.

To make the distinction clearer, I'll invent a way to ruin podcasting. Nobody do this, okay?

Some crummy person could make an app that transcribes all the podcasts available in a store and synthesizes a new "artificially intelligent" podcast that combines snippets from lots of different podcasts that—as one example—contain the same set of keywords. You could say, "I want to hear opinions about *x* political candidate," or maybe about some celebrity.

Then you'd hear a rapid-fire sequence of people saying things about the subject. You would *not* hear what had come just before each snippet or what comes next. The snippets would go by so fast, and there'd be so many of them, that even if a computer voice identified where each snippet was snipped from, you wouldn't be able to take it in.

Podcasters would strive to come up with snippets catchy enough to be snagged and rolled into the sausage. There would be a lot of goofy cursing, ambushes, freaky screams and laughs, none of which meant much.

AI researchers would proudly show how one podcaster's voice can be made to speak what another podcaster has said. You could get all your podcasts read by the actor of your choice. What Ezra Klein says, intoned by Gilbert Gottfried.

Plus, personal voicemail messages would be inserted into the queue, just to up your engagement; maybe that would be the only way to even hear your own messages.

Oh, and there would be ads mixed in. Your spouse's voice talking about that new internet-of-things sensor clothing that reports your posture to unknown targeted advertising services. In the middle of a mush of fragments of politics podcasts, a voice would talk about how a politician is running a child sex ring in the basement of a pizza parlor.

Armies of trolls and fake trolls would game the system and add enough cruel podcast snippets to the mix that your digest would become indigestible. Even the sweetest snippets would become mere garnishes on a cruel, paranoid, enraging, and crazy-making sonic soup.

Or, maybe your aggregated podcast will be a filter bubble. It will include only voices you agree with—except they won't really be voices, because the content will all be mushed together into a stream of fragments, a caricature of what listeners supposedly hold in common. You wouldn't even live in the same universe as someone listening to a different aggregation.

The podcast aggregator app might be called something AI-arrogant, like *Podcast Meta-genius*, or maybe something toddler-cute, like *Poddytraining*.

If this scenario sounds preposterous and bizarre, look at what has happened to text, image, and video already. How is *Poddytraining* different or worse than what people who rely on social media feeds to connect to the world already accept?

Podcasts still rely on stores and subscriptions, so they maintain a person-to-person structure instead of a person-to-crowd/algorithm/hidden-manipulator structure.

Enjoy podcasts while you can. Please stay alert, and if podcasts are ruined, stop making them and stop listening. For now, remember that you have only the most tenuous connection to the *meaning* of the stuff you add to the BUMMER monster.

SOCIAL MEDIA IS DESTROYING YOUR CAPACITY FOR EMPATHY

This argument is the flip side of the argument about how social media makes you meaningless. Other people are also becoming meaningless; you understand less about what's going on with *them*.

Recall that Component C of BUMMER—Cramming experiences into your life—means that algorithms determine what you see. That means you don't know what other people are seeing, because Component C is calculating different results for them. You can't know how much the worldviews of *other* people are being biased and shaped by BUMMER. Personalized search, feeds, streams, and so on are at the root of this problem.

Suppose an old-time behaviorist placed a row of caged dogs in a lab, each dog getting treats or electric shocks, depending on what that dog just did. The experiment would work only if each dog got stimuli tied to that dog's specific behavior. If the wires were crossed, so that dogs were getting each other's stimuli, then the experiment would cease to function.

The same thing is true of people in a BUMMER platform.

The implications for people are even more profound than for dogs, however, because the people aren't in separate cages, and therefore rely crucially on *social perception*.

This means that we notice one another's reactions in order to help us each get our own bearings. If everyone around you is nervous about something, you will get nervous, too, because something must be going on. When everyone is relaxed, you'll tend to relax.

When I was a kid, a common prank was to go to a place where there were other people and simply start looking up at the sky. Soon everyone was looking up at the sky, even though there was nothing there.

A wonderful way to notice social perception is to travel to a country where you don't speak the language. You'll find that you are suddenly very attuned to what other people are doing and what they are paying attention to, because that's the only way to know what's going on. One time I noticed people in a jungle in Thailand paying attention to a certain direction, so I did too, just in time to get out of the way of speeding army jeeps that came out of nowhere. Social perception saved my life. It has always been part of how humanity has survived.

But when we're all seeing different, private worlds, then our cues to one another become meaningless. Our perception of actual reality, beyond the BUMMER platform, suffers.

There are many recent examples, such as the time a person fired a shot in a pizza parlor because of a frenzied online belief that a child sex ring was being run out of the basement.[1] There were false beliefs spread by social craziness before BUMMER, such as those that inspired the Salem witch hunts, but acute outbreaks were rarer than they are today. The speed, idiocy, and scale of false social perceptions have been amplified to the

---

[1] https://www.snopes.com/pizzagate-conspiracy/

point that people often don't seem to be living in the same world, the real world, anymore.

This is another one of those obvious problems that sneaked up on us. Public space lost dimension, but also commonality in general has been desiccated.

A thought experiment can help expose how weird our situation has become. Can you imagine if Wikipedia showed different versions of entries to each person on the basis of a secret data profile of that person? Pro-Trump visitors would see an article completely different from the one shown to anti-Trump people, but there would be no accounting of all that was different or why.

This might sound dystopian or bizarre, but it's similar to what you see in your BUMMER feed. Content is chosen and ads are customized to you, and you don't know how much has been changed for you, or why.

Another way to see the problem is to think about public spaces. If you share a space with people who aren't looking at their smartphones, you are all in that space together. You have a common base of experience. It can be an amazing feeling, and it's a big reason why people go to clubs, sports events, and houses of worship.

But when everyone is on their phone, you have less of a feeling for what's going on with them. Their experiences are curated by faraway algorithms. You and they can't build unmolested commonality unless the phones are put away.

Traces of the old sharable world remain. You can watch the old-fashioned TV news that people like you watch, or that people who aren't like you watch. I don't like Fox News in the United States, for instance, because I think it's too paranoid, partisan, and cranky. But I watch it sometimes, and it helps me understand what other people who watch it are thinking and feeling. I cherish that ability.

I have no way of seeing your social media feed, however. I therefore have lessened powers to empathize with what you think and feel. We don't need to all see the same thing to understand each other. Only old-fashioned authoritarian regimes try to make everyone see the same thing. But we do need to be able to peek at what other people see.

Empathy[2] is the fuel that runs a decent society. Without it, only dry rules and competitions for power are left.

I might have been responsible for bringing the term "empathy" into high-tech marketing, because I started talking about VR as a tool for empathy back in the 1980s. I still believe that it's possible for tech to serve the cause of empathy. If a better future society involves better tech at all, empathy will be involved.

But BUMMER is precisely tuned to ruin the capacity for empathy.

DIGITALLY IMPOSED SOCIAL NUMBNESS

A common and correct criticism of BUMMER is that it creates "filter bubbles."[3] Your own views are soothingly reinforced, except when you are presented with the most irritating versions of opposing views, as calculated by algorithms. Soothe or savage: whatever best keeps your attention.

You are drawn into a corral with other people who can be maximally engaged along with you as a group. BUMMER

---

[2] Here I am using the term "empathy" to mean an ability to understand what other people are experiencing and why; to imagine one being in another's place. The term can mean different things at different times. When it entered the English language about a century ago, it was originally meant to convey the way a person might imagine it would feel to be any other part of the universe, like a mountain or a grape, which were two examples from the earliest thought experiments; it was a term of art for the aesthetic and psychological premonitions of virtual reality. See https://www.theatlantic.com/health/archive/2015/10/a-short-history-of-empathy/409912/

[3] https://www.penguinrandomhouse.com/books/309214/the-filter-bubble-by-eli-pariser/9780143121237/

algorithms intrinsically gravitate toward corralling people into bubbles, because to engage a group is more effective and economical than to up engagement one person at a time.

(But, to review, the term should be "manipulate," not "engage," since it's done in the service of unknown third parties who pay BUMMER companies to change your behavior. Otherwise, what are they paying for? What else could Facebook say it's being paid tens of billions of dollars to do?)

On the face of it, filter bubbles are bad, because you see the world in tunnel vision. But are they really new? Surely there were damaging and annoying forms of exclusionary social communication that predate BUMMER, including the use of racist "dog whistles" in politics.

For example, in the 1988 American presidential election, politicians famously used the story of a black man named Willie Horton who had committed crimes after a prison furlough in order to evoke latent racism in the electorate. But in that case, everyone saw the same ad, so you could at least get a sense of why someone else might have responded to it in a racist way, even if you strongly disagreed.

But now you don't always get to see those racist ads. This is sometimes because of so-called dark ads, which show up in a person's newsfeed even though they aren't technically published as news.[4] Many extremist political dark ads on Facebook only came to light as a result of forensic investigations of what happened in the 2016 elections.[5] They were blatant and poisonous, and Facebook has announced plans to reduce their harm, though that policy is in flux as I write.

While no one outside Facebook—or maybe even inside

---

[4] https://www.theguardian.com/technology/2017/jul/31/facebook-dark-ads-can
-swing-opinions-politics-research-shows
[5] https://www.forbes.com/sites/jaymcgregor/2017/07/31/why-facebook-dark-ads
-arent-going-away/

Facebook—knows how common or effective dark ads and similar messages have been,[6] the most common form of online myopia is that most people can only make time to see what's placed in front of them by algorithmic feeds.

I fear the subtle algorithmic tuning of feeds more than I fear blatant dark ads. It used to be impossible to send customized messages to millions of people instantly. It used to be impossible to test and design multitudes of customized messages, based on detailed observation and feedback from unknowing people who are kept under constant surveillance.

It might turn out that a certain font around someone's portrait on a certain day makes a small percentage of people trust that person just a little less. Maybe the same font showed up in a popular video about an unpleasant topic that same day. No one will ever know why the font has the effect it does, though. It's all statistical.

The results are tiny changes in the behavior of people over time. But small changes add up, like compound interest.

This is one reason that BUMMER naturally promotes tribalism and is tearing society apart, even if the techies in a BUMMER company are well meaning. In order for BUMMER code to self-optimize, it naturally and automatically seizes upon any latent tribalism and racism, for these are the neural hashtags waiting out there in everyone's psyche, which can be accentuated for the purpose of attention monopoly. (I'll address this problem in more detail in the argument about how social media makes social improvement hopeless.)

Not only is your worldview distorted, but you have less awareness of other people's worldviews. You are banished from the experiences of the other groups being manipulated sepa-

---

[6] https://slate.com/technology/2018/02/no-a-study-did-not-claim-that-fake-news-on-facebook-didnt-affect-the-election.html

rately. Their experiences are as opaque to you as the algorithms that are driving your experiences.

This is an epochal development. The version of the world you are seeing is invisible to the people who misunderstand you, and vice versa.

THE LOST THEORY IN YOUR BRAIN

The ability to theorize about what someone else experiences as part of understanding that person is called having a theory of mind. To have a theory of mind is to build a story in your head about what's going on in someone else's head. Theory of mind is at the core of any sense of respect or empathy, and it's a prerequisite to any hope of intelligent cooperation, civility, or helpful politics. It's why stories exist.

You've heard expressions like "Don't judge someone until you've walked a mile in their shoes." You can't understand people without knowing a little of what they've gone through.

Most animals get by without theory of mind, but people need it.

When you can only see how someone else behaves, but not the experiences that influenced their behavior, it becomes harder to have a theory of mind about that person. If you see someone hit someone else, for instance, but you did not see that they did it in defense of a child, you might misinterpret what you see.

In the same way, if you don't see the dark ads, the ambient whispers, the cold-hearted memes, and the ridicule-filled customized feed that someone else sees, that person will just seem crazy to you.

And that is our new BUMMER world. We seem crazy to each other, because BUMMER is robbing us of our theories of one another's minds.

Even when other people's experiences are candidly caught on camera, perhaps by a smartphone or a dashcam, BUMMER motivates enough noise to destroy commonality. BUMMER-driven opacity plays out online all the time. A video shows the moments before a police shooting, for instance, but BUMMER makes people upload endless versions of the video with different edits, overlays, and obfuscations. Empathy is lost to noise.

Trump supporters seem nuts to me, and they say liberals seem nuts to them. But it's wrong to say we've grown apart and can't understand each other. What's really going on is that we see less than ever before of what others are seeing, so we have less opportunity to understand each other.

Sure, you can monitor at least some of the typical content that other people are probably seeing. I keep up with conservative news sites, for instance. I always seek out personal contact with people who disagree with me if they're willing to give it a go.[7] There's even a nice community on Reddit devoted to this quest,[8] but it's drowned out by an ocean of chaotic poison.

The degree of difference between what is shown to someone else and what I can guess is being shown is itself unknowable. The opacity of our times is even worse than it might be because the degree of opacity is itself opaque. I remember when the internet was supposed to bring about a transparent society. The reverse has happened.

---

[7] Since I live in Berkeley, my town is periodically invaded by alt-right people who want to demonstrate. What astounds me is that several times men with conservative bumper stickers on their pickups have thrown nasty looks at me and my family, and they know nothing about us. Once, one of them swerved in a mock "Maybe I'll run you over" moment. If I could know what that driver had seen, then I would have a chance at empathy. It might be possible to talk. BUMMER has robbed us of that possibility.

[8] https://www.wired.com/story/free-speech-issue-reddit-change-my-view/

SOCIAL MEDIA IS MAKING
YOU UNHAPPY

WHY DO SO MANY FAMOUS TWEETS END
WITH THE WORD "SAD"?

The cheerful rhetoric from the BUMMER companies is all about friends and making the world more connected. And yet science reveals[1] the[2] truth.[3] Research[4] shows a world that is *not* more connected,[5] but instead suffers from a heightened sense of isolation.[6]

The pattern[7] has become so clear[8] that even research published by social media companies shows how they make you

---

[1] https://arxiv.org/abs/1408.3550

[2] https://papers.ssrn.com/sol3/papers.cfm?abstract_id=2886783

[3] http://journals.plos.org/plosone/article?id=10.1371/journal.pone.0069841

[4] https://academic.oup.com/aje/article-abstract/185/3/203/2915143

[5] http://rsos.royalsocietypublishing.org/content/3/1/150292

[6] http://www.ajpmonline.org/article/S0749-3797(17)30016-8/fulltext

[7] https://www.theguardian.com/technology/2017/may/01/facebook-advertising-data-insecure-teens

[8] http://www.sciencedirect.com/science/article/pii/S0747563214001241

sad. Facebook researchers have practically bragged[9] that they could make people unhappy without the people realizing why.[10]

Why promote something like that as a great research result? Wouldn't it be damaging to Facebook's brand image? The reason might have been that it was great publicity for reaching the true customers, those who pay to manipulate. The ones who are manipulated, meaning *you*, are the product, not the customer.

More recently, Facebook researchers finally acknowledged[11] what other researchers have found: that their products can do real harm.

What really bugs me about the way social media companies talk about this problem is that they'll say, "Sure we make you sad, but we do more good in the world than harm." But then the good things they brag about are all things that are intrinsic to the internet, that could—so far as we know—be had without the bad stuff, without BUMMER. Yes, of course it's great that people can be connected,[12] but why must they accept manipulation by a third party as the price of that connection? What if the manipulation, not the connection, is the real problem?[13]

At the start of this chapter I shared a few references about

---

[9] https://www.nytimes.com/2014/07/01/opinion/jaron-lanier-on-lack-of-transparency-in-facebook-study.html

[10] http://www.pnas.org/content/111/24/8788.full

[11] https://newsroom.fb.com/news/2017/12/hard-questions-is-spending-time-on-social-media-bad-for-us/

[12] https://slate.com/human-interest/2018/01/the-facebook-moms-group-that-has-helped-me-raise-kids-without-going-crazy.html

[13] Here's a study that detects both positive and negative effects of social media use and is able to characterize them: http://www.jahonline.org/article/S1054-139X(15)00214-1/abstract/. The connection aspect of social media was helpful to college-age women who were concerned about their weight, while the mutual ranking aspect was not. This result reinforces the hypothesis that the connections made possible by the internet can be positive, but that certain additional structures, typically emphasized by commercial social media, cause harm.

how social media makes you sad, even when connecting with people on the internet might otherwise make you happy, but the quantity of data is overwhelming. Just do a search. (Be aware that when you do that, it might have an impact on your feeds; you might be tagged—not necessarily explicitly, but implicitly, by association—as a potentially depressible person. Online manipulators might use algorithms that automatically try to take advantage of that, and it might make you depressed.)

Read the papers in the footnotes to dig into research that supports the thesis that social media makes you sad. You'll also find a variety of hypotheses about why it is so: the setting of unreasonable standards for beauty or social status, for instance, or vulnerability to trolls.

Why the variety? Wouldn't one way of bumming people out be enough? Since the core strategy of the BUMMER business model is to let the system adapt automatically to engage you as much as possible, and since negative emotions can be utilized more readily, of course such a system is going to tend to find a way to make you feel bad. It will dole out sparse charms[14] in between the doldrums as well, since the autopilot that tugs at your emotions will discover that the contrast between treats and punishment is more effective than either treats or punishment alone. Addiction is associated with *anhedonia*, the lessened ability to take pleasure from life apart from whatever one is addicted to, and social media addicts appear to be prone to long-term anhedonia.[15]

Of course BUMMER will make you unhappy. But how? The

---

[14] There are positive effects of social media in certain circumstances, of course. The overall effect on individuals and the world, however, is negative. A good journal for academic research on the topic is *Media Psychology*, published by Taylor and Francis: http://www.tandfonline.com/loi/hmep20/. A credible researcher in the employ of Facebook who highlights instances of positivity in social media is Moira Burke: http://www.thoughtcrumbs.com/.

[15] https://www.sciencedirect.com/science/article/pii/S0747563216302941

particular form of unhappiness will be tailored to you, as a matter of course. The people who run the BUMMER companies need never find out what brought you down. That is for you to know, your last privacy. You might become anxious that you're not as attractive or successful as other people you are exposed to, even as you're harnessed by the system to make someone out there feel the same way.

Based on the research, there are trends in the forms that unhappiness takes, so I could guess about what's going on with you. You might have less sex than you seek *in proportion* to the amount of time you use apps to seek sex.[16] You're sitting there swiping at a screen. You might spend less time with your family in proportion to the cuteness of the presentation of your family life you put out there on social media.[17] You might be at risk for self-harm in proportion to your social media use, especially if you're a young woman.[18] You might be making traumatic experiences worse by using social media.[19] You might be losing self-esteem even as you express yourself.[20]

I could guess, but that's not the approach I'm going to take here. I don't know you. Research only reveals statistical tendencies. You might be the exception. It's not my job to make guesses about what's right for you.

---

[16] https://www.eurekalert.org/pub_releases/2015-05/sdsu-caa050415.php

[17] http://annenberg.usc.edu/news/around-usc-annenberg/family-time-decreasing-internet-use

[18] https://www.theguardian.com/society/2017/sep/23/stress-anxiety-fuel-mental-health-crisis-girls-young-women

[19] http://www.pnas.org/content/pnas/early/2017/10/16/1708518114.full.pdf

[20] http://www.smh.com.au/technology/smartphone-apps/fuelling-a-mental-health-crisis-instagram-worst-social-network-for-young-peoples-mental-health-20170520-gw9fvq.html

THE WRONG END OF THE BUMMER

What I *will* do is dig into why I've found that certain online designs, including most social media, make me unhappy. My discontent is related to all the arguments that have come before, because BUMMER places me in a subordinate position. It's structurally humiliating.

What bums me out is not some particular surface pattern—like seeing everyone else misrepresent their lives as being more wealthy, happy, and trouble-free than they are—but instead it's the core BUMMER system. Being addicted and manipulated makes me feel bad, but there's more to it than that. BUMMER makes me feel judged within an unfair and degrading competition, and to no higher purpose.

I started to notice the bad feelings from the earliest prototypes of social media, which go way back to the 1980s. Even with ancient services like early Usenet, I found that there was a strange, unfamiliar hollow in me after a session. It was something I had not felt since I was a child. An insecurity, a feeling of not making the grade, a fear of rejection, out of nowhere.

I thought I must be at fault, because here was a more advanced technology, and surely that meant it was better than primitive analog media like telephones and newspapers.

This feeling was coincident with discovering my inner troll, which I described in the argument about assholes, but it could also be felt distinctly. I took an experimental approach to myself. If I felt bad after using an internet design, what were its qualities? How was it different from designs that left me happy? Here is one thing I discovered about myself: I don't mind being judged if the judges put in real effort, and a higher purpose is being honestly served, but I *really* don't like it when a crowd judges me casually, or when a stupid algorithm has power over me.

I don't like it when a program counts whether I have more or fewer friends than other people, whether people like me, or if I am in some way better, cooler, more likely to get rich, or whatever. BUMMER algorithms *must* put you into categories and rank you in order to do anything BUMMER at all. The whole purpose of BUMMER is turning you and changes to your behavior into a product. The algorithms fundamentally work to favor platform owners and advertisers, and those parties need abstractions of you in order to manipulate you.

The BUMMER algorithms behind companies like Facebook and Google are stored in some of the few files in the world that can't be hacked; they're kept *that* secret. The deepest secrets of the NSA[21] and the CIA[22] have leaked, repeatedly, but you can't find a copy of Google's search algorithm or Facebook's feed algorithm on the dark web.[23]

Part of the reason is that if everyone could see how present-day artificial intelligence and other revered cloud programs really worked, they would be alarmed. They'd realize how arbitrary the results can sometimes be. (This randomness was explored in the first argument.) The algorithms are only fractionally, statistically useful, and yet that thinnest thread of utility has built the greatest fortunes of our time.

But to me it's not even about the programs, however over-worshipped they might be, but about the power relationships that arise because people accept and implicitly respect the programs.

There have always been overblown—outright ridiculous—sources of information and opinions about you, but they didn't

---

[21] https://www.cbsnews.com/news/nsa-breach-shadow-brokers-michael-morell/
[22] https://www.theguardian.com/media/2017/mar/07/wikileaks-publishes-biggest-ever-leak-of-secret-cia-documents-hacking-surveillance
[23] You could add Trump's tax returns to this rarefied list.

use to matter much. An example was old-fashioned horoscopes in newspapers. There wasn't any way for a company to track your clicks or your eye gaze, so no one knew what you read. If you read your horoscope (which—I'm sorry if you're a believer—seems ridiculous to me) then so what?

Maybe you really believed in astrology, maybe you thought it was interesting to have random things said about you, or maybe you thought the whole thing was just a joke, but fun. Whatever. It was between you and an inanimate object, and maybe an occasional person you'd tell.

The horoscope in the newspaper didn't do anything outside of your own head; it did nothing that affected the power relationships between you and other people.

Things are different in the age of BUMMER. Let's say that instead of a paper newspaper, it's an online service, and let's say that instead of horoscopes, the judgments about you concern your health, your work ethic, your dating desirability, or something else. Facebook, for instance, puts you into categories based on your political leaning and many other factors.[24] These categories are BUMMER's answer to horoscopes.

The judgments of the BUMMER algorithms that classify you might not be meaningful or reliable in a scientific sense, but they really do matter in real life. They play into what news you see, whom you're introduced to as a potential date, what products you are offered. Judgments based on social media might determine what loans you can get,[25] which countries you can visit,[26] whether you get a job,[27] what education you can

---

[24] https://www.nytimes.com/2016/08/24/us/politics/facebook-ads-politics.html

[25] https://papers.ssrn.com/sol3/papers.cfm?abstract_id=2475265

[26] https://www.reuters.com/article/us-usa-immigration-visa/trump-administration
-approves-tougher-visa-vetting-including-social-media-checks-idUSKBN18R3F8

[27] https://www.forbes.com/sites/adp/2016/10/24/how-to-legally-use-social-media
-to-recruit/#1fd4ebce29f4

receive,[28] the outcome of your auto insurance claim,[29] and your freedom to congregate with others.[30] (In many of these examples, third parties are applying their own judging algorithms to BUMMER data instead of relying on the categories created by BUMMER companies directly.)

Your whims and quirks are under the microscope of powers greater than you for the first time, unless you used to live in a police state like East Germany or North Korea.

The inability to carve out a space in which to invent oneself without constant judgment; *that* is what makes me unhappy. How can you have self-esteem when that's not the kind of esteem that matters most anymore?

How can you find happiness without authentic self-esteem? How can you be authentic when everything you read, say, or do is being fed into a judgment machine?

To be clear, there are two levels of judgments going in the BUMMER machine. One kind can be understood by humans, and might be seen by humans. The internet is filled with opinions about you, you personally, right now. How many friends, followers? Are you hot? How many points have you earned? Did you get a virtual gold star or maybe some virtual confetti from a store because you convinced others to use the same store?

The other level of judgment is based on mathematical correlations that people might not ever see or be able to interpret. These are sometimes called intermediate-layer interpretations because of how they are generated within machine learning

---

[28] https://www.tuition.io/2014/04/social-media-shocker-twitter-facebook-can-cost -scholarship-admissions-offer/

[29] https://www.edmunds.com/auto-insurance/car-insurance-companies-use -facebook-for-claims-investigations.html

[30] https://www.theguardian.com/technology/2016/oct/11/aclu-geofeedia-facebook -twitter-instagram-black-lives-matter

algorithms. They are used to optimize BUMMER sneakiness: What ads are most likely to have a certain effect on you, what news, what cute cat pictures mixed into the feed of news you are getting from family members?

Whatever the details, notice what's happening. Suddenly you and other people are being put into a lot of stupid competitions no one asked for. Why aren't you sent as many cool pictures as your friend? Why aren't you followed as much? This constant dosing of social anxiety only gets people more glued in. Deep mechanisms in the social parts of our brains monitor our social standing, making us terrified to be left behind, like a runt sacrificed to predators on the savannah.

I realized a long time ago that I don't want to be ranked unless it's for something specific that I chose. If I want to get funding for a research project, I know I have to compete for it, and I know my project will be ranked. But how dare some crappy algorithm broadcast an unsought ranking of me?

But as ridiculous as it is, when it happens, I find I can't just put it out of my mind. There's some little demon in me that's competitive. Most of us probably have this creature inside us.

I see that so-and-so was just judged to be more popular/ intelligent/connected/valuable/whatever and that little demon inside me says, "Oh, yeah?" Then I feel I need to do something about it: either win at the game or find a different game.

But so long as you remain inside BUMMER, you can never escape. There are a million BUMMER games going on all the time, and you're a loser at almost all of them, because you're competing with the whole planet. The winners are mostly random.

It's as if, instead of one football game being played at a time, there's always a global game that takes up the whole earth, with everyone pitted against everyone and most of us always losing. Worst sport ever.

Even worse, there are a few people, Silicon Valley people like me, who are looking down on you, seeing more than you or your friends can, and manipulating you.

HIGH CASTLE

This truth really hit me one time when Google was new and small. I was over at their little pre-Googleplex offices and a friend of mine, one of their first programmers, told me about an email they had received from a woman who was very upset. Whenever someone Googled this woman's name, the first thing they saw was a moronic post that claimed she was obsessed with urine.

It was an interesting moment for Google's early crew. Should they heed the desperate demands of the woman to do something about her situation, or should they trust that in the bigger picture, the harm would be outdone by a greater good?

This sort of issue (pun!) is old news today, but unfortunately lives can still be ruined. Uber, which is pseudo-BUMMER, called the ability to spy on people the "God View."[31]

From the amazing godlike perspective of Silicon Valley, either people or algorithms can always see who has written what, and when; who looked it up and read it, and when. We can see the whole process as if we are looking in on an ant farm. And the little ants know it. They know they are being watched. The woman wrote increasingly impassioned pleas for

---

[31] https://www.forbes.com/sites/kashmirhill/2014/10/03/god-view-uber-allegedly
-stalked-users-for-party-goers-viewing-pleasure/

help. Some people in the office that day felt sorry for her, while some laughed at her.

That sense of being an ant watched by supposedly superior beings who are actually not superior at all, but just the same old people from school, just the ones who happened to get BUMMER jobs . . . that feeling is degrading and depressing.

And let me remind you that negative emotions are more readily accessible and more profitable BUMMER magnets for people than positive ones.

If ordinary people were to get all happy and satisfied, they might take a moment away from the obsession with social media numbers and go frolic in the flowers or even pay direct attention to each other. But if they're all on edge about whether they're popular enough, worried about whether the world is imploding, or furious at morons who are thrust into the middle of their connections with friends and families, then they dare not disengage. They are hooked because of provoked natural vigilance.

We in Silicon Valley like to watch the ants dig harder into their dirt. They send us money as we watch.

The imbalanced power relationship is in your face all the time. Don't you feel humiliated using one of the Facebook brands, like Instagram or WhatsApp? Facebook is the first public company controlled by one person.[32] I mean, I don't personally have anything against Mark Zuckerberg. It isn't about him. But why would you subordinate a big part of your life to *any* one stranger?

When I was growing up there were big politicians, rich people, pop stars, captains of industry, and all that, but none of them got to run my life in any substantial way. They influenced

---

[32] http://fortune.com/2016/04/27/zuckerberg-facebook-control/

me now and then by saying something that caught my attention, but that was it. They remained far away from my personal life.

I suspect that even though you might say it doesn't bother you, on some level you know it does, and there's no point in being angry because you can't see any way to do anything about it. But there is. Delete your accounts.[33]

[33] https://www.theguardian.com/media/2016/sep/21/does-quitting-social-media
-make-you-happier-yes-say-young-people-doing-it

SOCIAL MEDIA DOESN'T WANT YOU TO HAVE ECONOMIC DIGNITY

DOUBLE BUMMER

Since BUMMER showed up, the economic lives of many people in the developed world have taken on an uncomfortable quality. More and more people rely on the gig economy, which makes it hard to plan one's life. Gig economy workers rarely achieve financial security, even after years of work. To put it another way, the level of risk in their financial lives seems to never decline, no matter how much they've achieved. In the United States, where the social safety net is meager, this means that even skilled, hardworking people may be made homeless by medical bills, even after years of dedicated service to their profession.

Meanwhile, a small number of entrepreneurs—who always turn out to be close to some kind of computation hub—have become fantastically wealthy, creating an ever-widening gap between rich and poor, reminiscent of the nineteenth century's Gilded Age. Risk has been radiated out to ordinary people;

those close to the biggest computers are locked in to wealth, like casino owners.

Is this unsustainable shift in the economic/social contract related to BUMMER, or did the two developments just happen to appear at the same time? The answer is that BUMMER has not only made a lot of people emotionally insecure; it has also made many folks financially insecure.

What's the connection? To explain, I first need to tell you about digital politics in the years when BUMMER was born.

BABY BUMMER

BUMMER was in part an unintended consequence of an intense, almost religious movement to promote free and open software in the decade before the internet coalesced. Ironically, social and political pressure from techie hippies is what drove entrepreneurs to focus almost exclusively on ad-based business models when the internet happened.

Whatever else the BUMMER companies brought into the world, the feature that caught the public's imagination most in the beginning was probably that they were free. You didn't need to pay Google for a search or to upload or watch a video on YouTube; there was no fee to join Facebook or Twitter.

Being free is what propelled these services to become so big so fast. It is also the foundation of the BUMMER business plan that has been so destructive, that has turned most of the human race into part-time lab rats. (It's also why bad actors can afford to launch an unbounded number of fake people into the world.)

The notion of giving a high-tech information service away for free and making money with ads was not new. Back in the early decades of the twentieth century, there had not been any choice but to make over-the-air radio and TV free, because there was no way for a station to know who was tuning in. Who would you charge? Business plans have a way of sticking around even when they're obsolete, however. Note that the ads didn't go away when customers moved to paid cable.

In the case of internet services, there was a choice from the start. In fact, the very first design for a digital network, dating to Ted Nelson's work as a student in the 1960s, presumed that people would pay and be paid in tiny increments for goodies on a digital network. But that idea was pounded into virtual oblivion—albeit with the best of intentions—by the free-software movement.

The movement to make software free was founded on an honest mistake. It became dogma that if software wasn't free, then it couldn't be open, meaning no one but the owner would see the source code, so no one would understand what the software really did. To be fair, that concern wasn't based on speculation; companies that sold software typically didn't reveal source code. The reason was that if the source code was revealed, then it could be modified slightly and resold as a new program, which would deny sales to the original developer.

Everyone knew that software would eventually become more important than law, so the prospect of a world running on hidden code was dark and creepy. Therefore, the transparency that must underlie democracy, literacy, and decency was thought to be incompatible with any business model but free. Free and open would be forever bound together. But how would programmers make a living if their code was freely copied? Maybe they could give away the code and make money from being paid to solve problems that came up. They'd enter a gig economy instead of a royalty economy. They'd be laborers instead of accruing capital. But at least source code would remain visible, so an open, democratic society would flourish.

Nice sentiment, but it didn't work. In the era when activists first demanded that software be made open, the computers weren't connected yet. Now they are; they have been for decades. That means that a BUMMER company can build a model of you in software—and control what you see in a manipulative feed—by running programs exclusively *on their own computers*. Those computers are placed in super-secure locations you'll never visit. Their software is super-hyper secret. Every other kind of file has been breached by hackers, but not the search or feed algorithms of the big BUMMER companies. The secret code to manipulate you is guarded like crown jewels.

The software that matters most is the most hidden, the least revealed. Guess what? BUMMER software usually runs on a foundation of free and open software (like the Linux/Apache stack). But no one can know what is done on top of that free and open foundation. The open-software movement failed absolutely in the quest to foster openness and transparency in the code that now runs our lives.

Things could have turned out better. Now that the computers are connected, it is possible to imagine a collaboration tool that tracks where each line of code, each digital image, and every sound came from in a game, for example: to know who did what. That way, everyone who contributes to a collaborative development project could be paid in proportion to their contribution and how much the game is played. Letting someone else tweak your code would no longer mean that you wouldn't get paid for your work at all. We have failed to explore a world of possibilities.

CONFLICTED BUMMER

In the years before Google, the first major BUMMER company, was born, hippie techies were fearsome advocates of making everything information-related free, but that's not the only ideal they loved.

Techies also practically worshipped hero entrepreneurs like Steve Jobs. Tech business leaders were maybe not as smart as hackers, as far as hackers were concerned, but they were still considered visionaries. We *liked* it when they got rich. Who would want a future that was designed by some kind of boring government or committee-like process? Look at the smooth and shiny computers that Steve Jobs brought to the world!

So, two passions collided. Everything must be free, but we love mega tech founder heroes.

Do you see the contradiction? Everything is supposed to be free, but everything is also supposed to be about hero entrepreneurs, and entrepreneurs make money. How can those two directives be reconciled?

There was a lot of hedging and fudging on this point around the turn of the century. Ultimately, only one method of reconciliation was identified: the advertising business model. Advertising would allow search to be free, music to be free, and news to be free. (That didn't mean that musicians or reporters got a piece of the pie, for the techies considered them replaceable.) Advertising would become the dominant business in the information era.

This didn't feel dystopian at first. The original ads on Google were cute and harmless. But as the internet, the devices, and the algorithms advanced, advertising inevitably morphed into mass behavior modification.

This is how BUMMER was born. As often happens with

people, we forgot that we made a choice. Now we feel helpless. But the choice remains, and we can remake it.

BUMMER BLINDERS

The most dangerous thing about BUMMER is the widespread illusion that BUMMER is the only possibility. There are Silicon Valley people who believe that everything in the world can be reinvented/disrupted by tech startups. We'll disrupt medicine, education, transportation, even the cycle of life and death, but we have a blind spot about our basic method of operation. We have enshrined the belief that the only way to finance a connection between two people is through a third person who is paying to manipulate them. We feel locked into this certainty, but the trap is only in our heads.

Inherent in the BUMMER business model is the assertion that there is only one possible way for digital services to work, which is that you, the individual user, must be made subservient. That is not true. The prevalence of this message is one of the best reasons to quit social media.

The BUMMER idea is so pervasive that it soaks into unrelated businesses. We've taken as a fact of nature that if you want the benefits of an app like Uber—using the latest tech to improve coordination between drivers and people who need rides—then you must accept that a few people will mostly own Uber and some of them will become obnoxious oligarchs, while drivers will have less security than old-fashioned cab drivers, and riders will be spied upon in humiliating ways. None of these downsides need to occur to get the benefits. The only reason for the linkage is that we've been conditioned by BUMMER.

In some alternative universe—a universe we must build if we are to survive—there will be both the convenience of an app like Uber *and* a sustainable social and economic fabric in which a lot of people build security with dignity.

The fundamental commercial product of BUMMER is absurd and deleterious. You can't make a society wealthy by making it crazy. The only way out is to change the business model so that today's BUMMER companies can make money in a different way. That will chart the way for other companies like Uber that rely on similar cloud services and personal devices to adopt sustainable, dignified business models. And they can!

BETTER THAN BUMMER

One way is to directly monetize services such as search and social media. You'd pay a low monthly fee to use them, but if you contributed a lot—if your posts, videos, or whatever are popular—you could also earn some money. A large number of people, instead of the tiny number of token stars in the present system, would earn money. (I acknowledge, of course, that there would have to be a way of making services available to those who couldn't afford to pay even a small fee.)

I'm making a fuss about the potential to earn because a system like this would help address looming losses of employment due to AI and automation. We're talking about an industry that supports some of the richest companies the world has ever known, and it's all driven by data that comes from people who are often being told that they're about to be obsolete, that they'll need to go on the public dole with a basic income system. It just isn't right to tell people they are no longer valuable to society when the biggest companies exist only because of data that comes from those same people.

For instance, consider language translation. It's great that we have automatic translations of memos and web pages, say between English and Chinese. But there isn't some self-sufficient digital brain behind the scenes that delivers these translations.

Instead, tens of millions of fresh phrase translations need to be gathered every single day from real people who don't know that data is being taken from them. How is it being taken? Vast numbers of bilingual individuals translate phrases all the time as part of their BUMMER activity, perhaps to annotate a foreign TV show for their friends. Anything you do on BUMMER is fair game, as far as the BUMMER companies are concerned.

Translated phrases are matched to new phrases that other people want to have translated, and a statistical mash-up of these correspondences produces a generally readable text in another language. The new translation examples have to be gathered every day because languages are alive. Every day brings new events, pop culture, and slang.

It's wonderful that this technology works, but what's not wonderful is that the people who are supplying the data that make it work—real, biological, bilingual humans—have become insecure. Human translators have suffered a loss of career prospects that mirrors what happened to investigative journalists, recording musicians, photographers, and others.

We're pretending that the people who know how to translate are obsolete, when in truth they're still needed. Isn't it some kind of sin to tell someone that they're obsolete when it isn't true?

What we call AI should never be understood as an alternative to people, but instead as a mislabeled new channel of value *between* real people.

The business plan of BUMMER is to sneakily take data from you and make money off it. Look at how rich BUMMER companies are and remember that their wealth is made entirely of the data you gave them. I think companies *should* get rich if they make things people want, but I don't think you should be made less and less secure as part of the bargain. Capitalism isn't supposed to be a zero-sum game.

BUMMER is economically unsustainable, which is even worse, perhaps, than its being unfair. Bringing down a society to get rich is a fool's game, and Silicon Valley is acting foolishly.

Once we acknowledge that a translation program needs data from real people, then those people might even be encouraged to provide better, more useful data. The people might be valued honestly, might get paid, and might feel a sense of earned dignity. The translation service might then perform better! The fantasy of human obsolescence not only undervalues people, but often makes supposed AI programs less functional because no one is motivated to improve the underlying data.

The stupidity of the BUMMER approach to human value transcends economic unsustainability; it is a breach of human dignity. That dimension will be explored in the tenth argument, on spiritual concerns.

BUMMER was originally sold as a barter deal. "Let us spy on you and in return you'll get free services." This might seem like a reasonable deal in the short term, but in the long term it's terrible.

The free services that you get are disguised versions of services someone like you would otherwise be paid to provide. Musicians use BUMMER to promote themselves for free, and yet a smaller percentage of musicians are doing well enough to plan families—which is a reasonable definition of "security"— than during the era when music was sold on physical discs.[1] Recording musicians; language translators . . . who's next?

Before the BUMMER era, any time a new technology came

---

[1] I defended this claim in my previous books *You Are Not a Gadget* and *Who Owns the Future?*

along that made a set of human roles obsolete, new roles appeared that were less physical. *Car drivers instead of horsemen*. Indeed, the new roles that came into being because of tech disruptions were often more creative and professional than the old ones. *Robotics programmers instead of ironworkers*. This meant that more and more people gained prestige and economic dignity.

BUMMER reversed the trend. Now, if you bring insight, creativity, or expertise into the world, you are on notice that sooner or later BUMMER will channel your value through a cloud service—probably a so-called AI service—and take away your financial security, even though your data will still be needed. Art might be created automatically from data stolen from multitudes of real artists, for instance. So-called AI art creation programs are already practically worshiped. Then, robotic nurses might run on data grabbed from multitudes of real nurses, but those real nurses will be working for less because they're competing with robotic nurses.

Everyone is feeding BUMMER data because they're addicted and trapped by network effects, as described in the first argument.

In the argument about how BUMMER is making you into an asshole, I suggested that bringing in some level of reward system beyond clannish mind games can inspire dignity in online relations. I suggested LinkedIn as one example of how economic engagement, instead of purely social engagement, can have a civilizing effect.

This hypothesis needs to be tested more, but it is possible that when we enter into a new era in which people are paid for the value their data brings to the online world, then that world will become less dark and crazy.

The above sketch of an alternate business model for what are now BUMMER services like social media and search is only one possibility. I suspect there are others. This particular idea was pitched in a book of mine called *Who Owns the Future?* Lately, this approach to the future of digital economics has become known as "Data as Labor."[2]

DaL has gained traction in economics circles and is surely worth further exploration. It won't be perfect, but it will be better than BUMMER.[3]

THE CORP PERSPECTIVE

The BUMMER companies should not fear a transition to a non-BUMMER business plan. It will be better for them!

I'm not anti-Google, for instance, even though I have philosophical disagreements with some people there. My buddies and I sold a startup to Google and I enjoyed many days hanging out in the small, nascent seed of Google. I don't think Google considered as a set of people has turned evil, even if its business plan has.

I often hear that Google and Facebook will never change their business models because the BUMMER model is so successful that shareholders won't allow it. I disagree.

One problem with the BUMMER model is that it's like oil for a petrostate. A BUMMER-dependent company can diversify its activities—its cost centers—all it wants, but it can never diversify its profit centers, because it always has to prioritize free services in order to grab more data to run the manipulation services. Consumers are addicted, but so are the BUMMER empires.

BUMMER makes tech companies brittle and weirdly

---

[2] https://papers.ssrn.com/sol3/papers.cfm?abstract_id=3093683/; https://www.economist.com/news/finance-and-economics/21734390-and-new-paper-proposes-should-data-providers-unionise-should-internet

[3] Some internet sites that might have gone BUMMER are flirting with the subscription model: https://mobile.nytimes.com/2017/05/20/technology/evan-williams-medium-twitter-internet.html.

stagnant. Of the big five tech companies, only two *depend* on the BUMMER model. Apple, Amazon, and Microsoft all indulge in a little BUMMER, but they all do just fine without depending on BUMMER. The non-BUMMER big tech companies have successfully diversified. There are plenty of reasons you might want to criticize and change those three companies, but the amount of BUMMER they foster is not an existential threat to civilization.

The two tech giants that are hooked on BUMMER, Google and Facebook, are *way* hooked. They make the preponderance of their profits from BUMMER despite massive investments in trying to start up other types of businesses. No matter the scale, a company based on a single trick is vulnerable. Sooner or later some disruption will come along, and then a BUMMER company, no matter how large, will quickly collapse.

So why is it again, that BUMMER is such a great long-term strategy for tech companies? It isn't. It trades the short term against the long term, just like a petrostate.

Instead of trying to shut down BUMMER companies, we should ask them to innovate their business models, for their own good.

THE USER PERSPECTIVE

It might sound undesirable to someday have to pay for things that are currently free, but remember, you'd also be able to make money from those things. And paying for stuff sometimes really does make the world better for everyone. Techies who advocated a free/open future used to argue that paying for movies or TV was a terrible thing, and that the culture of the future would be made of volunteerism, with the digital distribution funded by advertising, of course. This was practically a religious belief in Silicon Valley when the big BUMMER companies were founded. It was sacrilege to challenge it.

But then companies like Netflix and HBO convinced people to pay a monthly fee, and the result is what is often called "peak TV." Why couldn't there also be an era of paid "peak social media" and "peak search"?

Watch the end credits on a movie on Netflix or HBO. It's good discipline for lengthening your attention span! Look at all those names scrolling by. All those people who aren't stars made their rent by working to bring you that show.

BUMMER only supports stars. If you are one of those rare, rare people who are making a decent living off BUMMER as an influencer,[4] for instance, you have to understand that you are in a tiny club and you are vulnerable. Please make backup plans! I hate raining on dreams, but if you think you are *about* to make a living as an influencer or similar, the statistics are voraciously against you, no matter how deserving you are and no matter how many get-rich-quick stories you've been fed.[5] The problem isn't that there are only a few stars; that's always true, by definition. The problem is that BUMMER economics allow for almost no remunerative roles for near-stars. In a genuine, deep economy, there are many roles. You might not become a pro football player, but you might get into management, sports media, or a world of other related professions. But there are vanishingly few economic roles adjacent to a star influencer. Have a backup plan.

When social media companies are paid directly by users instead of by hidden third parties, then they will serve those users. It's so simple. Someone will be able to pay to see poisonous

[4] https://www.cbsnews.com/news/social-media-influencers-brand-advertising/
[5] https://news.vice.com/en_ca/article/8xmmb4/what-does-it-take-to-make-a-living
-on-social-media

propaganda, but they won't be able to pay to have that poison directed at someone *else*. The incentive for poisoning the world will be undone.

I won't have an account on Facebook, Google, or Twitter until I can pay for it—*and* I unambiguously own and set the price for using my data, and it's easy and normal to earn money if my data is valuable. I might have to wait a while, but it'll be worth it.

SOCIAL MEDIA IS MAKING
POLITICS IMPOSSIBLE

ARC BURN[1]

There used to be a moral arc to history, pointed out by Martin Luther King Jr.; justice got broader over time. In one period, slaves were freed; in another women got the vote; in another LGBTQ people gained rights and respect. Democracy spread to more and more countries.

Just recently, in the age of BUMMER, the arc is showing signs of crashing to the ground and burning. There are not just backlashes as we climb the arc, but unthinkable, catastrophic falls.

In recent years Turkey, Austria, the United States, India,

---

[1] This is a chapter about politics. Before going any further, I have to say something obvious. This is a vital topic and I've seen a side of it you probably haven't, so I want to tell you about that. At the same time, I'm a white techie, but in order to proceed I must talk about things I can't know as well as I know my own world, like the black experience in America. I'm probably going to fall into the traps of whitesplaining, mansplaining, techsplaining, or other forms of 'splaining. Can we just stipulate that that's true? I'm sure it is. Please take what you can use from me. I know I don't know everything.

and other democracies have elected authoritarian-leaning leaders who rely on tribalism for their power. Voters are choosing to negate themselves. In each case, BUMMER played a prominent role. I hope, dearly, that our times will be remembered as a momentary glitch in a previously smooth progression toward a more democratic world.

But for the moment we face a terrifying, sudden crisis. Before the BUMMER era, the general thinking was that once a country went democratic, it not only stayed that way but would become ever more democratic, because its people would demand that.

Unfortunately, that stopped being true, and only recently.[2] Something is drawing young people away from democracy. Despite all the hopeful self-congratulations from social media companies, it seems that when democracy has been weakened, the online world has just gotten ugly and deceitful.

The correlation might be even stronger in developing regions. Simple access to information technology, like the ability to send texts with phones, has probably contributed to the marvelous and historic reduction in abject poverty around the world in the past few decades. But more recently, commercial social media showed up, and phones turned into propagators of maniacal social violence.

One of the world's great human rights catastrophes is the plight of the Rohingya population of Myanmar. As it turns out, this crisis corresponded to the arrival of Facebook, which was quickly inundated by shitposts aimed at the Rohingya.[3] At the same time, viral lies about child abductions, in that case mostly on Facebook's WhatsApp,

---

[2] https://www.weforum.org/agenda/2017/06/millennials-are-rapidly-losing-interest
-in-democracy/

[3] https://www.nytimes.com/2017/10/29/business/facebook-misinformation-abroad
.html

have destabilized parts of India.[4] According to a United Nations report, social media is also a massively deadly weapon, literally, in South Sudan—because of shitposts.[5]

Mysterious authors flood social media feeds with bizarre claims of wrongdoing—variations of the blood libel—supposedly perpetrated by a targeted group. Memes to stimulate genocide often report something horrible that is said to have been done to children. As always with BUMMER, the nastiest, most paranoid messaging gets the most attention, and emotions spiral out of control as a byproduct of engagement spiraling out of control.

All of these regions had problems before. History is filled with weird, bad, or crazy politicians. It is also filled with mass hysterias and violent mob delusions. And countries that fail. Are we really in exceptional times?

It will only be possible for future historians to make that call. It seems to me that something has gone bad and dark in our world, and suddenly so, just in recent years, with the arrival of BUMMER. It's not that we're seeing unprecedented horrors— they have precedents—but that the precious arc of improvement has reversed. We're backsliding terribly and suddenly.

A typical story of social media in politics goes like this: A group of hip, young, educated people gets into a social media platform first, because these things come out of the hip, young, educated world. They're idealistic. They might be liberal, conservative, or anything. They sincerely want the world to be better. That goes for both the techies who make a BUMMER platform and the people out in the world who use it.

---

[4] https://www.washingtonpost.com/world/asia_pacific/indias-millions-of-new
-internet-users-are-falling-for-fake-news%E2%80%94sometimes-with-deadly
-consequences/2017/10/01/f078eaee-9f7f-11e7-8ed4-a750b67c552b_story.html

[5] http://www.securitycouncilreport.org/atf/cf/%7B65BFCF9B-6D27-4E9C-8CD3
-CF6E4FF96FF9%7D/s_2016_963.pdf

They meet early successes, often spectacular, ecstatic successes, but then the world turns sour, as if by magic. BUMMER ultimately fuels loudmouthed assholes and con artists more than it does the initial groups of hip, young, educated idealists, because in the longer term BUMMER is more suited to sneaky, malevolent manipulation than to any other purpose.

BUMMER studies early idealists and catalogs their quirks by its very nature, without an evil plan. The results have the unintended effect of lining idealists up so that they can be targeted with shitposts that statistically make them just a little more irritable, a little less able to communicate with dissimilar people, so a little more isolated, and after all that, a little less able to tolerate moderate or pragmatic politics.

BUMMER undermines the political process and hurts millions of people, but so many of those very same people are so addicted that all they can do is praise BUMMER because they can use it to complain about the catastrophes it just brought about. It's like Stockholm syndrome or being tied to an abusive relationship by invisible ropes. The sweet, early idealists lose, all the time thanking BUMMER for how it makes them feel and how it brought them together.

ARAB SPRING

The Arab Spring was an occasion for hearty self-congratulation in Silicon Valley. We claimed it as our glory at the time. "Facebook Revolution" and "Twitter Revolution" were common tropes back then.[6]

We gathered in front of big screens watching kids in Tahrir

---

[6] http://www.nytimes.com/2012/02/19/books/review/how-an-egyptian-revolution
-began-on-facebook.html

Square in Cairo taking on a despotic government and we were in love. We celebrated as ordinary citizens used social media to tell NATO forces where to target air strikes. Social media put a modern army at the fingertips of ordinary social media users.

There had been revolutions before, but something was different this time.

There wasn't any particular charismatic figure, for instance. There was no George Washington or Vladimir Lenin. Here, we thought, was a revolution truly of the people. There were no generals hunched over big tables with maps as underlings scurried around them. There was no unifying manifesto, no general agreement or even particularly focused discussion about what would come after the revolution. The term "democracy" was thrown around, but there was little discussion about what it meant. Democracy was confused with a thin faith that online collective dynamics would lead to a better world. A self-organized revolution could do no wrong. Here, we thought, was the realization of our faith in networks.

I wasn't so sure. Some of my friends got pissed at me when I asked, "Where are those kids going to get jobs?" Or even worse, "Is Twitter or Facebook going to get those kids jobs?" I also complained that a revolution belonged to those accomplishing it, and it was wrong to bring in the brand names of Silicon Valley companies.

Well, no one got them jobs, and indeed no one was around to coherently claim power in Egypt other than theocratic extremists, who were then ousted by a military coup, and almost none of the inspiring young people who protested have decent jobs.

What social media did at that time, and what it always does, is create illusions: that you can improve society by wishes alone; that the sanest people will be favored in cutting contests; and that somehow material well-being will just take care of itself.

What actually happens, always, is that the illusions fall apart when it is too late, and the world is inherited by the crudest, most selfish, and least informed people. Anyone who isn't an asshole gets hurt the most.

So I was the cynic, but it turned out I wasn't even close to being cynical enough. No one wants to associate their tech company brand with what happened next.

There had been reactions against revolutions before, as well as hijacking of revolutions, corruptions of revolutions, reigns of terror, and many other dysfunctions. But something was different this time.

A widespread phenomenon of networked nihilistic terror exploded.[7] Young people were watching the most awful, sadistic videos, channeled to them by Silicon Valley companies, and the dynamic was like porn. Kids became addicted to atrocity. That had certainly happened all too often before, but in the past it had been organized. Gangs had ruled history's many killing fields, but now, loners were "self-radicalizing."

A lonely male persona became familiar, strutting in a made-up world, bounded by the pettiest of illusions, filled with insecure rage.

But Silicon Valley's faith in social media as a tool for social improvement was not even tarnished. It still lives in me. As I write, on New Year's Day 2018, the Iranian regime is blocking social media to suppress protests erupting around the country. An inner voice in me rises up: "Yes! Yes, online technology is helping people organize and they'll be clever enough to route around attempts to shut them out."

I don't want to give up that hope. None of us do. But the evidence thus far is not encouraging.

---

[7] https://www.wired.com/2016/03/isis-winning-social-media-war-heres-beat/

GAMERGATE

I was heartened when women started to speak up in the gaming community. The gaming world is wonderful in a lot of ways, but it really isn't meeting its potential. Gaming should be turning into the new way we learn and talk about complicated issues. That's happening to a small extent, but the biggest productions tend to target the same demographic over and over again. You've got guns, you're traversing terrain, and you're shooting at something. Over and over. The industry needs to spread its wings more.

Developers who thought gaming should broaden in this way made use of social media to communicate their ideas, and created a vibrant, distributed movement. They earned attention and you could feel the atmosphere shift a little. Many of those developers were female.

What happened next was a rich-world version of what had happened with the Arab Spring. The reaction was astonishingly extreme and ugly, of a different order than the thing it was reacting against.

Women who talked about gaming were attacked in vicious ways that have since become terribly normal. They were bombarded with fake images of themselves and their families being murdered, raped, and so on.[8] Their personal details were posted, forcing some women to go into hiding.[9]

The movement to destroy critics of the gaming world was called "Gamergate." It's impossible to talk to anyone who supports it, because they live in an alternate universe of conspiracy

---

[8] http://www.dailymail.co.uk/news/article-4858216/Victim-Gamergate-s-horrific
-online-abuse-reveals-trauma.html
[9] http://time.com/3923651/meet-the-woman-helping-gamergate-victims-come-out
-of-the-shadows/

theories and dense jungles of stupid arguments fueled by the pettiest of illusions, bursting with insecure rage.

Gamergate became a feeder and model for the alt-right.[10]

LGBTQ

In the years immediately before the 2016 election in the United States, laws around LGBTQ issues started to change. Same-sex marriage was legalized, trans people were more out and accepted. Social media undoubtedly played a role.

But that was only the first stage in the process of BUM-MER degradation. That was the BUMMER honeymoon. Well-meaning people won a historically smooth round in the fight, and it felt as if any level of improvement in society you could dream of was in easy reach.

It's like a heroin high, as that has been described to me; an incredible, easy, early burst of ecstasy, after which you're inevitably going down, catastrophically.

The next stage in BUMMER politics is the one in which assholes realize they're favored by BUMMER. All kinds of assholes appear. They get enough attention to outpace the well-meaning people who just won victories. They exhume horrible prejudices and hatreds that haven't seen the light of day for years, and they make those hatreds mainstream.

Then it turns out that even bigger assholes manipulate the early-adopter assholes. Then big bad things start to happen. Horrific, giant assholes get elected, stupid xenophobic projects are elevated, ordinary people suffer horrible, needless material losses, and wars loom.

In the case of the United States, astonishingly extreme

---

[10] http://www.zero-books.net/books/kill-all-normies

anti-LGBTQ figures were elevated to the highest offices[11] even though LGBTQ dignity and rights issues were untouchable in terms of argument during the election itself.

It's not that BUMMER disfavors LGBTQ people. BUMMER could care less. It's that it favors con artists and assholes. These are Components A and F, the wind in BUMMER's sails.

NEITHER LEFT NOR RIGHT, BUT DOWN

BUMMER is neither liberal nor conservative; it is just pro-paranoia, pro-irritability, and pro–general assholeness.

Remember, BUMMER isn't that way *at first*. At first, nice early-adopter people seem to get a boost. However, once those nice people have been categorized, algorithmically probed and tested, and readied for manipulation, *then* the assholes take over.

Who cares if I myself am liberal? If you are a principled conservative, do you think you've really been well served by BUMMER? My evangelical Christian conservative friends suddenly find themselves wedged into social media communities that support an obscene, cruel philanderer and abuser who made fortunes from gambling and bankruptcies and who has stated, on the record, that he doesn't need or seek forgiveness from God.[12] Meanwhile my patriotic, hawkish conservative friends now find themselves aligned with a leader who would almost certainly not be in office were it not for cynical, illegal interventions by a hostile foreign power. Look what BUMMER has done to your conservatism.

The same thing happens to liberals. Remember Bernie Bros? Remember how it became cool in some liberal circles to cruelly

---

[11] https://transequality.org/the-discrimination-administration
[12] https://www.washingtonpost.com/news/acts-of-faith/wp/2016/06/08/trump-on
-god-hopefully-i-wont-have-to-be-asking-for-much-forgiveness/

ridicule Hillary, as if doing so were a religion? In the age of BUMMER you can't tell what was organic and what was engineered.[13]

It's random that BUMMER favored the Republicans over the Democrats in U.S. politics, but it isn't random that BUMMER favored the most irritable, authoritarian, paranoid, and tribal Republicans.[14] All those qualities are equally available on the left. If a U.S. version of Hugo Chavez had come along, he could have been president. Maybe it will happen in the future. Yuck.

As a lefty, I don't think a BUMMER-style lefty leader would be any better than Trump. Debasement is debasement, whatever direction it comes from.

The ways that a "disaster artist" candidate can be preferred by Facebook are well known, though the details remain opaque. When a candidate, or any other customer, buys access to user attention through Facebook, the amount of access isn't just determined by how much is spent, but by how well Facebook's algorithms determine the customer is *also* promoting and increasing the use of Facebook. People who worked on the social media strategy of the Trump campaign have claimed[15] that Trump gained *hundreds of times* more access[16] for a given spend than did the Clinton campaign, though Facebook claims that wasn't so, without revealing enough to make the story transparent.[17] If there *was* a multiplier, it probably applied as much to Russian

---

[13] https://www.rawstory.com/2017/03/russians-used-bernie-bros-as-unwitting-agents-in-disinformation-campaign-senate-intel-witness/

[14] https://www.vox.com/policy-and-politics/2018/2/24/17047880/conservatives-amplified-russian-trolls-more-often-than-liberals

[15] https://www.wired.com/story/how-trump-conquered-facebookwithout-russian-ads/

[16] Brad Parscale, the Trump campaign's social media director, tweeted: "I bet we were 100x to 200x her. We had CPMs that were pennies in some cases. This is why @realDonaldTrump was a perfect candidate for FaceBook."

[17] https://slate.com/technology/2018/03/did-facebook-really-charge-clinton-more-for-ads-than-trump.html

operatives and other pro-Trump parties buying access on Facebook as to the Trump campaign making direct purchases. The algorithms can't care and don't care.

An interesting detail that came out a year after the election is that Facebook had offered both the Clinton and Trump campaigns onsite teams to help them maximize their use of the platform, but only Trump's campaign accepted the offer.[18] Maybe if Clinton had agreed to have Facebook employees in her office, she would have won. The election was so close that any little thing that moved the needle in her direction could have tipped the result.

Facebook and other BUMMER companies are becoming the ransomware of human attention. They have such a hold on so much of so many people's attention for so much of each day that they are gatekeepers to brains.

The situation reminds me of the medieval practice of indulgences, in which the Catholic Church of the time would sometimes demand money for a soul to enter heaven. Indulgences were one of the main complaints that motivated Protestants to split off. It's as if Facebook is saying, "Pay us or you don't exist."

They're becoming the existential mafia.

BLACK LIVES MATTER

After a dramatic series of awful killings of unarmed black citizens by police in the United States, the initial reaction from sympathetic social media users was for the most part wise, stoic, and constructive. It must be said that we might not even have heard much about these killings, their prevalence, or their similarities without social media.

---

[18] https://www.cbsnews.com/news/facebook-embeds-russia-and-the-trump-campaigns-secret-weapon/

At first, social media engendered a universal sense of community. The slogan "Black Lives Matter" initially struck me as remarkably knowing and careful, for instance. Not a curse, not a swipe. Just a reminder: our children matter. I suspect that a lot of people got the same impression, even though many of them would come to ridicule the same slogan not long after.

"Black Lives Matter" appeared and gained prominence during the typical honeymoon phase of BUMMER activism, and, as always, that early phase was hopeful and felt substantial. BUMMER was giving black activists a new channel to influence and power. More money and power for the BUMMER companies, for sure, but also more empowerment for new armies of BUMMER users. Win/win, right?

But during that same honeymoon, behind the scenes, a deeper, more influential power game was gearing up. The game that mattered most was out of sight, occurring in algorithmic machinery in huge hidden data centers around the world.

Black activists and sympathizers were carefully cataloged and studied. What wording got them excited? What annoyed them? What little things, stories, videos, anything, kept them glued to BUMMER? What would snowflake-ify them enough to isolate them, bit by bit, from the rest of society? What made them shift to be more targetable by behavior modification messages over time? The purpose was not to repress the movement but to earn money. The process was automatic, routine, sterile, and ruthless.

Meanwhile, automatically, black activism was tested for its ability to preoccupy, annoy, even transfix other populations, who themselves were then automatically cataloged, prodded, and studied. A slice of latent white supremacists and racists who had previously not been well identified, connected, or empowered was blindly, mechanically discovered and cultivated, initially only for automatic, unknowing commercial gain—but that would have been impossible without first cultivating a slice of BUMMER black activism and algorithmically figuring out how to frame it as a provocation.

BUMMER was gradually separating people into bins and promoting assholes by its nature, before Russians or any other client showed up to take advantage. When the Russians did show up, they benefited from a user interface designed to help "advertisers" target populations with tested messages to gain attention. All the Russian agents had to do was pay BUMMER for what came to BUMMER naturally.

"Black Lives Matter" became more prominent as a provocation and object of ridicule than as a cry for help. Any message can be reframed to incite a given population if message vandals follow the winds of the algorithms. Components F and A, locked together.

Meanwhile, racism became organized over BUMMER to a degree it had not been in generations.

I wish I didn't have to acknowledge this heartbreak. A lot of what goes on *at a user-to-user level* in BUMMER is wonderful if you look at it while ignoring the bigger picture in which people are being manipulated *by* BUMMER. If you can draw a small enough frame to include only the stuff that people are directly aware of on BUMMER, then it often looks exquisite.

Black Twitter is a great example. It's a distinct medium and literature unto itself. Black Twitter is marvelously inventive and expressive. And virtuosic. Black Twitter has run rings around Trump, such as after the "NFL kneeling scandal." Meanwhile, the stuff outside of a Twitter user's frame of awareness is intensely favored to continue to subsume Black Twitter and make it powerless.

I want to celebrate Black Twitter because it's brilliant. But I need to point out it's a cruel trap. Something similar to Black Twitter will hopefully exist someday that isn't subservient to

BUMMER and won't be fundamentally designed to secretly study people in order to manipulate them.

I want to be wrong about all this stuff, but so far BUM-MER looks worse and worse as more is revealed.

A year after the election, the truth started to trickle out. It turns out that some prominent "black" activist accounts were actually fake fronts for Russian information warfare. Component F. The Russian purpose was apparently to irritate black activists enough to lower enthusiasm for voting for Hillary. To suppress the vote, statistically.

That doesn't mean that Russians placed thoughts into people's heads in any clear or reliable way. It doesn't mean that the people targeted by these campaigns were any less thoughtful, intelligent, or strong-willed than anyone else. Most of what happened was probably the "redlined" promotion of cynicism, a dismissive attitude, and a sense of hopelessness ("redlining" refers to a sneaky way that U.S. banks historically biased creditworthiness algorithms to disfavor black neighborhoods). I am not saying that critiques of Hillary were invalid, or that voter sentiment was uninformed; I am saying that voter emotion was tweaked just a bit, enough to lower voter turnout.

Don't forget that Facebook had already noisily published research proving it can change voter turnout.[19] In the published research, Facebook used the cheerful example of boosting voter turnout. But since Facebook is all about targeting and can calculate your political affiliation, among many other things,[20] and since it has also proven it can make people sad,[21] it is likely that social networks can also be used to suppress

[19] http://www.nature.com/news/facebook-experiment-boosts-us-voter-turnout-1 .11401

[20] http://dailycaller.com/2016/08/24/facebook-is-determining-your-political -affiliation-tracks-your-activity/

[21] http://www.pnas.org/content/111/24/8788.full

voters who have been targeted because of how they are likely to vote.

None of this means that Facebook prefers one kind of voter to another. That's up to Facebook's customers, who are not you, the users. Facebook doesn't necessarily know what's going on. A social media company is in a better position if it doesn't know what's going on, because then it makes just as much money, but with less culpability.

We will never know what algorithmic tests took place in the service of voter suppression or activation in any particular election, or what lessons were learned. Maybe certain words in headlines, or placement of certain ads adjacent to certain celebrity news, turned out to improve the chances of making someone irritable, but only if they liked certain cars.

All we can surmise is that a statistically driven enterprise adapted continuously in order to optimize its performance.

Neither BUMMER nor Russian agents had to care about actual black activism, one way or another. (As it happens, the individuals who work at BUMMER companies tend to be liberal and are probably mostly sympathetic to black activism, but that's utterly irrelevant to their effect upon the world so long as they adhere to the mass manipulation business model.)

BUMMER makes more money when people are irritated and obsessed, divided and angry—and that suited Russian interests perfectly. BUMMER is a shit machine. It transforms sincere organizing into cynical disruption. It's inherently a cruel con game.

Black activists have every reason to feel good about their immediately perceptible interactions on BUMMER; there is genuine beauty and depth on that level. This other behind-the-scenes game doesn't make the visible game invalid. The only way in which looking at the whole picture matters is in observing and understanding the ultimate results.

Activists might feel confident they are getting their message out, but it is indisputable that black activists have severely lost ground politically, materially, and in every way that matters outside of BUMMER.

As usual, after an algorithmically prompted catastrophe, many of the people who have been betrayed and used like fools can only praise BUMMER.

One example of Component F in the 2016 U.S. election was an account called Blacktivist, which was run by the Russians. A year after the elections, the true power behind Blacktivist was revealed and reporters asked genuine black activists what they thought about it.[22] Some, fortunately, still had access to outrage. One activist reportedly said, "They are using our pain for their gain. I'm profoundly disgusted." That is an informed, reasonable statement, and a brave one, for it is not easy to accept that one has been tricked.

People tend to rationalize. For instance, a civil rights attorney told the same reporter, "If someone is organizing an event that benefits accountability and justice, I don't really care what their motives are or who they are." This is a typical rationalization from someone who does not look outside the frame of familiar experience at the larger picture where the game of BUMMER is played out.

At the end of the day, BUMMER moneymaking caused black social media to unintentionally elevate a new tool optimized for voter suppression. As if there weren't enough voter suppression tools out there already. As if gerrymandering, inaccessible polling stations, and biased registration rules weren't enough.

A lot of potential Hillary voters were infused with a not-great

---

[22] https://www.theguardian.com/world/2017/oct/21/russia-social-media-activism-blacktivist

feeling about Hillary, or about voting at all. Were you one of them? If so, please think back. Were you seeing any information customized for you before the election? Did you use Twitter or Facebook? Did you do a lot of online searches?

You were had. You were tricked. Your best intentions were turned against you.

IF ONLY THIS GAME WERE ALREADY OVER

Even if the current atmosphere—our hell of insults and lies— has started to seem normal,[23] it really wasn't like this before. I worry about young people growing up in our mess and believing this is how things always are.

While I was writing this book, a new social movement known as #metoo arose, announcing a rejection of sexual harassment of women. BUMMER algorithms are devouring everything about #metoo right now, as I type. How can it be turned into fuel to empower some asshole somewhere to annoy someone else in order to make everyone more engaged/manipulated? How will activists be goaded into becoming less sympathetic? What prospects will be discovered by manipulator/advertisers who are trawling/trolling to find ways to ruin the world?[24]

---

[23] Italian voters have favored a political party that has NO quality other than being BUMMER through and through: https://www.nytimes.com/2018/02/28/world/europe/italy-election-davide-casaleggio-five-star.html.

[24] Shortly before the first edition of this book went to the printer, a horrifying school shooting took place at a high school in Florida, and BUMMER was right there, as it always is, probing for ways to damage society: https://www.wired.com/story/pro-gun-russian-bots-flood-twitter-after-parkland-shooting/.

SOCIAL MEDIA HATES YOUR SOUL

I MET A METAPHYSICAL METAPHOR

The previous nine arguments exposed a web of patterns within and between people that has been disrupted by BUMMER.

To review: Your understanding of others has been disrupted because you don't know what they've experienced in their feeds, while the reverse is also true; the empathy others might offer you is challenged because you can't know the context in which you'll be understood. You're probably becoming more of an asshole, but you're also probably sadder; another pair of BUMMER disruptions that are mirror images. Your ability to know the world, to know truth, has been degraded, while the world's ability to know you has been corrupted. Politics has become unreal and terrifying, while economics has become unreal and unsustainable: two sides of the same coin.

All these dyads form a web of change in the human condition. That web is so encompassing that we must go back to the first argument and ask whether the explanatory metaphor it proposed was too timid. The first argument proposed that BUMMER users are trapped in addictive behavior-modification apparatuses. This is the metaphor that some of the founders of BUMMER have chosen to frame their regrets, and the pieces fall in place within that framing. It is useful. But is it adequate?

Behavior-modification cages can only manipulate one creature at a time, but when the whole society is being manipulated in a coordinated way, we must seek a grander explanatory framework. There aren't many choices. The clearest one is probably religion.

Each of the arguments for deleting your accounts is at first glance about a practical issue, such as trust, but on closer inspection, the arguments confront the deepest and most tender concerns about what it means to be a person.

When you use BUMMER, you implicitly accept a new spiritual framework. It is like the EULA agreement—the user agreement—that you clicked "OK" on without reading. You have agreed to change something intimate about your relationship with your soul. If you use BUMMER, you have probably, to some degree, statistically speaking, effectively renounced what you might think is your religion, even if that religion is atheism. You have been inducted into a new spiritual framework.

I am not speaking rhetorically or being cute. This is a sincere effort to illuminate what is happening.

THE FIRST FOUR PRINCIPLES OF BUMMER SPIRITUALITY

Let's reconsider the first four arguments in spiritual terms.

The first argument is about free will. Free will is a mysterious idea; a leap of faith. Does it even make sense? Maybe there is no free will; maybe it is an illusion. But religions generally propose that free will is real. It must exist in order for you to choose to change your karma for the better, or to make moral choices that get you into heaven. Even the most ethereal Buddhist must start with free will in order to freely seek a state that transcends it.

Free will can feel old-fashioned. Cutting-edge nerdy philosophers, engineers, and revolutionaries have been challenging it for centuries now.

Why not conceive of people as naturally evolved machines, but machines nonetheless? People could then be programmed to behave well, and the human project could flourish. Behaviorists, Communists, and now Silicon Valley social engineers have all tried to achieve that end.

But each time a nerd attempts to remove free will from the stage, it pops up with amplified concentration in a new spot. With the same breath that proclaims that communal algorithms or artificial intelligence will surpass individual human creativity, an enthusiast will inevitably exclaim that a Silicon Valley entrepreneur, AI programmer, or ideologue is a visionary who is changing the world, denting the universe (in Steve Jobs's phrase), and charting the future.

The ritual of engaging with BUMMER initially appears to be a funeral for free will. You give over much of your power of choice to a faraway company and its clients. They take on a statistical portion of your burden of free will, so that it is no longer in your purview. They start to decide who you will know, what you're interested in, what you should do. But it is no secret that the people who run the scheme have concentrated astonishing wealth and power in a ridiculously short amount of time. They have power, but how could power exist if free will does not?

So BUMMER intrinsically enacts a *structural*, rather than an ontological, change in the nature of free will. It will continue to exist, if under a barrage of insults. The important change is that you now have less free will, and a few people whom you don't know have more of it. Some of your free will has been transferred to them. Free will has become like money in a gilded age.

This change transcends economics and politics; it is the stuff of those religions that have proposed that only leaders have a mandate from heaven.

The second argument delineated a specific problem of concern, a structure that I dubbed BUMMER. My purpose was to identify a well-bounded target for change instead of falling into despair about everything in modernity. This structure turned out to be less a set of technologies than it was a business plan that spewed perverse incentives.

Another similarity to religions? Maybe my objection to BUMMER is like when Protestants objected to indulgences. There is a long history of people rejecting a structure connected with a religion while not rejecting the core.

If the BUMMER theory is right, then the overall project of the internet is not at fault. We can still enjoy the core of it. BUMMER wants you to think that without BUMMER there would be no devices, no internet, no support groups to help you through hard times, but that is a lie. It is a lie you celebrate and reinforce when you use BUMMER, just as someone who attends a corrupt church is supporting its corruption.

The third argument is about becoming an asshole. Remember that the idea is not that you become an asshole to everyone all the time, but that your Solitary/Pack switch is set to Pack. You focus on dynamics within the pack and between packs. You become an asshole to members of other packs and those below you in your pack hierarchy, and sometimes to competitive peers in the pack.

All you have to do is look at the role of religion in the conflicts around the world, at this or other times, to see that this dynamic also plays out in religions. Indeed, a common pattern today—with examples sadly given in the argument on politics—is that BUMMER resurrects old conflicts that had been associated with religion in order to "engage" people as intensely as possible.

Argument Four was about undermining truth, so it's a biggie from a spiritual point of view.

A strict religion might demand that adherents believe certain things that are not supported by evidence, or that are countered by it. Some religious people still think the sun orbits around the earth, for instance.[1]

Believing something only because you learned it through a system is a way of giving your cognitive power over to that system. BUMMER addicts inevitably at least tolerate a few ridiculous ideas in order to partake at all. You have to believe sufficiently in the wisdom of BUMMER algorithms to read what they tell you to read, for instance, even though there's evidence that the algorithms are not so great.[2] You must accept preposterous conspiracy theories in order to avoid being trolled in much of the world of BUMMER. You need to hold a worldview that dismisses whatever group of people you've been counterpoised with by engagement algorithms.[3]

---

[1] http://www.independent.co.uk/news/world/middle-east/saudi-muslim-cleric-claims-the-earth-is-stationary-and-the-sun-rotates-around-it-10053516.html

[2] https://weaponsofmathdestructionbook.com/

[3] The best-known quote from the alt-right writer "Mencius Moldbug" goes: "In many ways nonsense is a more effective organizing tool than the truth. Anyone can

I've been using both the term "spiritual" and the term "religious," and here's why: Religions generally are connected with specific truth claims, while spirituality might not be. Spirituality can usually coexist a little more easily with Enlightenment thinking.

The Enlightenment emphasized ways of learning that weren't subservient to human power hierarchies. Instead, Enlightenment thinking celebrates evidence-based scientific method and reasoning. The cultures of sciences and engineering used to embrace Enlightenment epistemology, but now they have been overridden by horribly regressive BUMMER epistemology.

You probably know the word "meme" as meaning a BUMMER posting that can go viral. But originally, "meme" suggested a philosophy of thought and meaning.

The term was coined by the evolutionary biologist Richard Dawkins. Dawkins proposed memes as units of culture that compete and are either passed along or not, according to a pseudo-Darwinian selection process. Thus some fashions, ideas, and habits take hold, while others become extinct.

The concept of memes provides a way of framing everything non-nerds do—the whole of humanities, culture, arts, and politics—as similar instances of meme competition, mere subroutines of a higher-level algorithm that nerds can master. When the internet took off, Dawkins's ideas were in vogue, because they flattered techies.

There was a ubiquitous genre of internet appreciation from the very beginning in which someone would point out the viral spread of a meme and admire how cute that was. The genre exists to this day. Memes started out as a way of expressing

believe in the truth. To believe in nonsense is an unforgeable demonstration of loyalty. It serves as a political uniform. And if you have a uniform, you have an army."

solidarity with a philosophy I used to call cybernetic totalism that *still* underlies BUMMER.

Memes might seem to amplify what you are saying, but that is always an illusion. You might launch an infectious meme about a political figure, and you might be making a great point, but in the larger picture, you are reinforcing the idea that virality is truth. Your point will be undone by whatever other point is more viral. That is by design. The architects of BUMMER were meme believers.

In the *very* big picture, virality might indeed be truth. Believing in memes does turn to truth, but only eventually— *very* eventually. If humanity destroys itself because malicious memes prevent us from dealing with climate change, for instance, then eventually, in a hundred million years, a species of intelligent octopus will take over and perhaps come across our remains and wonder what went wrong.

Rationality is different from evolution. It's faster. We don't know how rationality works, however.

There is something going on in the mind beyond memes. Our ability to conquer mystery is still a mystery. This can be a difficult truth to accept, apparently, and some techies prefer to live in denial.

Here are some tough truths: We currently don't have a scientific description of a thought or a conversation. We don't know how ideas are represented in a brain. We don't know what an idea is, from a scientific point of view. That doesn't mean we never will understand these things scientifically, just that we don't yet understand them. We can pretend that we will understand them any minute, so it is as if we already understand them, but then we are just lying to ourselves.

When we talk about politics, culture, art, or law, it's possible that quantity can't replace quality, even though we can't say what quality is. It's possible that the algorithms we know how to write simply can't distinguish terrorists or foreign intelligence agents from normal people who aren't trying to destroy the world.

The foundation of the search for truth must be the ability to notice one's own ignorance. Acknowledging ignorance is a beautiful feature that science and spirituality hold in common. BUMMER rejects it.

Virality is truth for BUMMER politics, BUMMER art, BUMMER commerce, and BUMMER life.

I've examined the first four arguments in more fundamental terms than before. I won't go through all ten; the principle that BUMMER is replacing the features of spirituality with its own designs is demonstrated enough in these examples. But I must dig deeper.

BUMMER FAITH

Not all questions can be addressed by evidence. So having faith about them is not a rejection of evidence. Religions at their best address the deepest, most important, and most tender questions that we can't approach scientifically, like the ultimate purpose of life, why existence exists, what consciousness is, what death is, and the nature of meaning.

In order to use BUMMER, you gradually acquiesce to BUMMER's answers to these questions. And BUMMER does provide answers: terrible ones! This is the quality of BUMMER that might piss me off the most.

The purpose of life, according to BUMMER, is to optimize. According to Google: "Organize the world's information." But per the typical Silicon Valley worldview, everything is information. Matter will be hacked, the human body will be hacked, and so on. Therefore, Google's mission statement reads, within tech culture, as "Organize all reality." That's why Google started all those weird Alphabet companies. You might not have thought about Google's worldview or mission, but you buy into it when you optimize your presence to rank high in search or optimize your video for views. The purpose of your life is now to optimize. You have been baptized.[4]

Usually Google has had a way of coming up with the creepier statements, but Facebook has pulled ahead: A recent revision in its statement of purpose includes directives like assuring that "every single person has a sense of purpose and community."[5] A single company is going to see to it that every single person has a purpose, because it presumes that was lacking before. If that is not a new religion, I don't know what is.

Google famously funded a project to "solve death."[6] This is such a precisely religious pretension that I'm surprised the religions of the world didn't serve Google with a copyright infringement take-down notice.[7] Google could have framed its work as life extension, or as aging research, but instead it went right for the prize, which is being the master of that which is most sacred within you. BUMMER must own you in order to own anything at all.

Facebook also plays the game. The Facebook page of a deceased person becomes a shrine that one can only visit as a member, and to be a member you must implicitly become an adherent.

Google's director of engineering, Ray Kurzweil, promotes the idea that Google will be able to upload your consciousness into the company's cloud, like the pictures you take with your smartphone. He famously ingests a whole carton of longevity

---

[4] The BUMMER ethos has bled into academic science as well. Young scientists must now chase citation numbers in the same way that aspiring social media influencers must seek followers.

[5] http://www.businessinsider.com/new-facebook-mission-statement-2017-6

[6] http://time.com/574/google-vs-death/

[7] The project continues as Calico, one of the Alphabet companies.

pills every day in the hope that he won't die before the service comes online. Note what's going on here. The assertion is not that consciousness doesn't exist, but that whatever it is, Google will own it, because otherwise, what could this service even be about?

I have no idea how many people believe that Google is about to become the master of eternal life, but the rhetoric surely plays a role in making it seem somehow natural and proper that a BUMMER company should gain so much knowledge and power over the lives of multitudes.

This is not just metaphysics, but metaphysical imperialism. If you buy into any of this stuff, explicitly or just through practice, you cannot even call yourself an atheist or agnostic. You are a convert.

BUMMER HEAVEN

One of the reasons that BUMMER works the way it does is that the engineers working at BUMMER companies often believe that their top priority among top priorities isn't serving present-day humans, but building the artificial intelligences that will inherit the earth. The constant surveillance and testing of behavior modification in multitudes of humans is supposedly gathering data that will evolve into the intelligence of future AIs. (One might wonder if AI engineers believe that manipulating people will be AI's purpose.)

The big tech companies are publicly committed to an extravagant "AI race" that they often prioritize above all else.[8] It's

---

[8] http://www.nationmultimedia.com/technology/Google-makes-machine-learning -artificial-intellige-30273758/; https://www.cnbc.com/2017/08/02/microsoft-2017 -annual-report-lists-ai-as-top-priority/; https://www.fastcompany.com/3060570 /facebooks-formula-for-winning-at-ai-/; https://www.reuters.com/article/us-amazon -com-reinvent-ai/amazon-steps-up-pace-in-artificial-intelligence-race -idUSKBN1DV3CZ

completely normal to hear an executive from one of the biggest companies in the world talk about the possibility of a coming singularity, when the AIs will take over. The singularity is the BUMMER religion's answer to the evangelical Christian Rapture. The weirdness is normalized when BUMMER customers, who are often techies themselves, accept AI as a coherent and legitimate concept, and make spending decisions based on it.[9]

This is madness. We forget that AI is a story we computer scientists made up to help us get funding once upon a time, back when we depended on grants from government agencies. It was pragmatic theater. But now AI has become a fiction that has overtaken its authors.

AI is a fantasy, nothing but a story we tell about our code. It is also a cover for sloppy engineering. Making a supposed AI program that customizes a feed is less work than creating a great user interface that allows users to probe and improve what they see on their own terms—and that is so because AI has no objective criteria for success.

Who is to say what counts as intelligence in a program? Back in the 1990s, my friends and I made the first programs that could track a person's face to turn it into an animated rendering of a creature or another person making the same expressions in real time. It didn't occur to us to call that AI. It was just an example of fancy image processing. But now, that capability is often called AI.

All kinds of different programs might or might not be called AI at a given time, so when a program is called AI, the inevitable result is that the criteria for success become vague. AI is a role-playing game for engineers, not in itself an actual technical achievement.

---

[9] https://komarketing.com/industry-news/ai-digital-transformation-top-marketers-priorities-2018/

Many of the algorithms that are called AI are interesting and actually do things, of course, but they would be better understood—and might even work better—without the AI storytelling. I gave an example of this in the argument on economics. People who translate between languages are being told they're becoming obsolete. Not only are they losing their livelihoods, but they are being robbed of dignity, because the narrative of their obsolescence is a lie. They are still valuable. They are needed because without their manually created data, there would be no "automatic" translation service.

EXISTENCE WITHOUT BUMMER

It's almost impossible to write about the deepest spiritual or philosophical topics, because people are on such hair triggers about them, but it would be a cop-out to avoid declaring a statement of beliefs regarding the basic questions that BUMMER is trying to dominate. I hope this statement will come off as rather generic and uncontroversial, though hoping doesn't make things so.

I am conscious. I have faith that you are also conscious. We each *experience*.

It's a marvel. I don't think of experience as either natural or supernatural. I don't know enough to know whether those are the only choices.

We can study brains, but we don't know whether a brain necessarily has to experience in order to do anything else. Experience is a mystery, deeper than other mysteries, because we know of no way to break it into parts to study it. We don't know whether it makes sense to talk about particles of experience (which some people call "qualia").

We can find in the existence of experience a thread of hope that there's an afterlife, but the mere fact that we experience while alive is no proof. Even so, it is not irrational to base faith or hope for an afterlife on the mysterious existence of internal experience in this life. None of us really knows what's going on in our strange situation of reality, but if you perceive a sense of positivity, of grace and progressive creativity in the world, then perhaps experience connects to more.

We can acknowledge experience, we can enjoy it, we can have an emotional reaction to the mystery of it, perhaps even a pleasant one. Acknowledging that experience exists might make us kinder, since we understand people to be more than machines. We might be a little more likely to think before hurting some-one if we believe there's a whole other center of experience cloaked in that person, a whole universe, a soul.

BUMMER ANTI-MAGIC

Should machines be given "equal rights," as is so often proposed in tech culture? Indeed, Saudi Arabia has granted citizenship to a "female" robot, and with that citizenship, rights not available to Saudi human women.[10]

This is a big problem with human-machine equivalence. Imagine a metaphorical circle of empathy that informs your actions. Within your circle are those you accept and humanize. If you make your circle too wide, it is diluted; you make your empathy absurd and become blind to how you are hurting real people. The Saudis are not the only ones who promote empathy for mute props as a way to deny empathy to real but muzzled humans. It's also been done in the name of anti-abortion activism[11] and animal rights.

---

[10] https://www.washingtonpost.com/news/innovations/wp/2017/10/29/saudi-arabia -which-denies-women-equal-rights-makes-a-robot-a-citizen/

[11] Here is an old piece that describes how I reconcile my views on the specialness of people with my support of abortion rights: https://www.huffingtonpost.com/entry /the-latest-innocent-embry_b_8547.html

The BUMMER business is interwoven with a new religion that grants empathy to computer programs—calling them AI programs—as a way to avoid noticing that it is degrading the dignity, stature, and rights of real humans.

Consciousness is the only thing that isn't weakened if it's an illusion. You'd have to experience the illusion in order for the illusion to exist. But the flip side of that is that if you choose not to notice that you're experiencing, you can negate your own consciousness.

You can make your own consciousness go poof. You can disbelieve in yourself and make yourself disappear. I call it anti-magic.

If you design a society to suppress belief in consciousness and experience—to reject any exceptional nature to personhood—then maybe people can become like machines.

That's happening with BUMMER. The BUMMER experience is that you're just one lowly cell in the great superorganism of the BUMMER platform. We talk to our BUMMER-connected gadgets kind of as if they're people, and the "conversation" works better if we talk in a way that makes us kind of like machines. When you live as if there's nothing special, no mystical spark inside you, you gradually start to believe it.

If this new challenge to personhood were only a question of spiritual struggle within each person, then perhaps we could say it is each person's responsibility to deal with it. But there are profound societal consequences.

Spiritual anxiety is a universal key that explains what might otherwise seem like unrelated problems in our world. Modernity is most often presented by BUMMER technologists as an assault on human specialness, and people naturally react in horror, as if they might be negated. It is a rational response because it is a response to what has actually been said.

The issues that are tearing the United States apart are all

about whether people are special, about where the soul might be found, if it is there at all. Is abortion acceptable? Will people become obsolete, so that everyone but a few elite techies will have to be supported by a charitable basic income scheme? Should we treat all humans as being equally worthy, or are some humans more deserving of self-determination because they are good at nerdy tasks? These questions might all look different at first, but on closer inspection they are all versions of the same question: What is a person?

Whatever a person might be, if you want to be one, delete your accounts.

CONCLUSION:
CATS HAVE NINE LIVES

I hope this book has helped you become a cat, but please be aware that I haven't included *all* the arguments about social media that you should consider; I haven't even come close. I have only presented arguments for which I have an uncommonly informed perspective or expertise.

This book doesn't address problems related to family dynamics, to untenable pressures placed on young people, especially young women (please read Sherry Turkle on those topics), the way scammers can use social media to abuse you, the way social media algorithms might discriminate against you for racist or other horrible reasons (please read Cathy O'Neil on that topic), or the way your loss of privacy can bite you personally and harm society in surprising ways. This book only scratches the surface. Remember, I'm a cat.

It might seem strange that a Silicon Valley denizen like me would be asking you to resist us. When you engage with us, when you resist creatively, you counter other forces, the bizarre financial incentives I've described, that already constrain us. In a way, your resistance can help free us. I am not asking for opposition, I am asking for help.

The best way you can help is not to attack those who would manipulate you from afar, but simply to free yourself. That will redirect them—us—and make us find a better way to do what we do.

How can you survive without social media? I don't know you, so I can't say—and there will probably be some innovation required—but in general: Don't reject the internet; embrace it! The internet itself is not the problem.

You don't need to give up friends: Email your friends instead of using social media, but use accounts that aren't read by the provider—so no Gmail, for instance. No need for a sneaky company between you and your friends.

You can still get news online: Read news websites directly (instead of getting news through personalized feeds), especially sites that hire investigative reporters. Get a feel for the editorial voice of each site, which is only available when you go direct. Subscribe to great news sites! Read three a day and you'll be better informed than social media users, and in less time. Consider using browser extensions that block the comments.

You won't stew in the dark: If you want to find things to do, look up local culture and events websites; there are usually wonderful ones run by dedicated local people. Start your own website!

You can even still watch YouTube videos, for now at least, without a Google account. Watching without an account and with some privacy plugins will give you access to a much less manipulative experience.

Sounds like work, right? But no matter how much effort you put in, you'll probably still save time overall by taking control of your own life. You'll be amazed to discover how much of your time was taken up before by BUMMER schemes.

Quit 'em all! Instagram and WhatsApp are still Facebook and still scoop your data and snoop on you. Don't tweet about how you quit Facebook or post to Facebook about how you quit Twitter.

Your goal should not necessarily be to force governments to regulate or even nationalize Facebook before you'll rejoin, or to force Facebook to change its business model, even though those are achievements that must precede the long-term survival of our species. Your immediate goal is to be a cat.

It's like learning to write. You can't read well until you can write at least a little. The reason we teach writing to students is not in the hopes that they'll all become professional writers. That would be too cruel. Instead, we hope they'll learn what it means to write, and to think, which will make them more thoughtful when they read. You can't use the internet well until you've confronted it on your own terms, at least for a while. This is for your integrity, not just for saving the world.

It's unlikely that there will be a vast wave of people quitting social media all at once; the combination of mass addiction with network-effect lock is formidable. But as more people become aware of the problems, they—you—can speak to the hearts of the tech industry and have an impact. If you drop accounts even for a while, it helps.

There's a deeper truth. Change is hard, but by offering good-natured pressure, you will be giving techies help we secretly need and even want. Techies can become isolated through extreme wealth and might seem unreachable, but actually we miss you. It doesn't feel good to be separated from society. When techies engage with fixing problems they helped create, they become connected again, and that feels good. If you can find a way to challenge us without vilification, it's good for us. Taking charge of your own information life is a great way to do that.

To conclude, I must remind you that the goal here isn't to convince you of what to think or what to do. It is not my job to change you, any more than it should be a BUMMER company's job. However, unless and until you know yourself, even you won't have standing to argue about what's right for you. And you can't know yourself unless you go to the trouble to experiment a bit.

I realize that we live in a world of stunning inequality, and not everyone has the same options. Whoever you are, I hope you have options to explore what your life might be, especially if you are young. You need to make sure your own brain, and your own life, isn't in a rut. Maybe you can go explore wilderness or learn a new skill. Take risks. But whatever form your self-exploration takes, do at least one thing: detach from the behavior-modification empires for a while—six months, say? Note that I didn't name this book *Arguments for Deleting Your Social Media Accounts Right Now and Keeping Them Deleted Forever*. After you experiment, you'll know yourself better. Then decide.

AN AFTERWORD IN THREE PARTS

Part One: Bleakest Teens

A question from high school students brought me to tears. These were the brightest students you could imagine; they had competed in a statewide contest to be able to ask me and a few other tech figures questions at an event. The first question, agreed to by all of them, was this:

"If artificial intelligence is going to surpass people in our lifetimes, if we won't have jobs, if the future doesn't need us, why did our parents have us? Why are we here?"

I like talking to teens and have heard plenty of rage, darkness, and cynicism, but never anything so bleak. Their eyes were stone.

How to respond?

"Oh my, you know AI isn't what it seems to be. It's just a way of people helping people, like any other technology. Remember, AI is just fancy statistics on data, and the data comes from you. You are the AI. It's just that under the present system, your data is taken without pay so it feels like this new creature, the AI, is a real entity, but it isn't. If we had a system where your contributions were recognized, then you wouldn't feel that you're going to be obsolete."

"But how can you say that? All the people are becoming interchangeable. We're just accounts to be swapped in and out by the big tech platforms. We're driving for Uber for only a short while until the cars drive themselves. All the new jobs feel that way. They're designed to go away easily. The tech industry says the AI race is an all-or-nothing race.[1] People are nothing more than 'hacks' companies can use for a little while longer until the machines get good enough. Then we'll sit around and get high while we watch our species fade away."

"You've been presented with that view your whole lives. All the bleak science fiction tells you that and the constant experience of being just another account, classified by social media algorithms, tells you that. There are news reports every day from the big tech companies that treat AI as a sort of new species instead of just a way of dressing up human effort. But logic tells us that the other way of thinking, in which AI isn't even a thing, is just as valid. It's hard to invert your worldview after a lifetime, but for the sake of your self-worth, you have to at least try."

We techies enjoy the most perverted economic incentive in history. We've convinced humanity that people are worth less than our machines, or will be soon. We own the machines; they don't. Our wealth will be infinite.

But what to say to these high school kids? It felt like my argument wasn't working. After a few rounds back and forth I started to lose it. "You matter to *me*. I look at you and I see the future I won't be around to see directly. You are the only reason I do anything. You will form the world my daughter lives in,

---

[1] https://techonomy.com/2019/03/youre-not-already-ai-youre-behind/

and all our descendants. You *must* find meaning and optimism. It is a duty not just to yourselves but to everyone." Well, what I said would have been more halting and broken than that.

No luck. "But you're just another meaningless human, about to be obsolete. You can't give us meaning."

Part Two: The Most Awful People and Crashing Planes

While this book says it's about social media, the social media companies perceive themselves to be in an AI race above all else, so ultimately this book must also be about AI, as was revealed in the tenth argument.

Please try a mental experiment. Consider the day's news and see whether it makes better sense if you use the trend of self-abnegation through belief in AI as an explanation for what is going on.

As I write this, for instance, one prominent news story is about a massacre in mosques in New Zealand. The shooter was steeped in the usual social media poison, the same stuff you are led to if you let the giant platforms recommend what to watch, which this week includes his live streaming of the killings, which the platforms seem unable to block.

Social-media inflected jihadists and white supremacists are the people who respond most to the way algorithms seek engagement and influence. The algorithms invoke fight-or-flight emotions and play on infantile needs for attention. The algorithms are programming everyone in a statistical distribution; the atrocity committers are those who are programmed the most keenly.

But I wonder if there's something deeper going on as well. Hannah Arendt and more recent thinkers like Masha Gessen point out that aimless, rootless, unfulfilled people are the fuel of authoritarian dysfunction. If the most lucrative business of the world is the AI race, which gives machines meaning at the expense of people, then that is a recipe for global authoritarianism.

The killer in New Zealand wrote a manifesto that began with the repeated invocation of an idea that is held in common by many of the worst people of our time. He wailed about his fear of being "replaced." For white nationalists, it is nonwhites who are doing the replacing, and not just immigrants. White nationalists chanted "Jews will not replace us" in a notorious event that took place in Charlottesville, Virginia, in 2017, even though there is little Jewish immigration in the United States.[2]

Leaving aside the racism, this fear is not based on facts.[3] There is no actual threat to the continued existence of a vast "white" or Caucasian-appearing population. I wonder, and I ask you to wonder, whether hearing that people will soon be made obsolete by AI—and hearing it from the richest and most lauded institutions in our society[4], over[5] and over[6]—might be contributing to an ambient fear of "replacement."

Remember, in every case in which AI can be touted as having replaced or surpassed people, you can just as easily reframe the situation as one in which people are being inventive and working together in new ways by using computers. The inclusion of the idea of AI, of a nonhuman actor, is entirely a matter of preference, though it does come with an economic benefit to whoever owns the supposed AI.[7]

---

[2] https://www.washingtonpost.com/news/acts-of-faith/wp/2017/08/14/jews-will-not-replace-us-why-white-supremacists-go-after-jews/?utm

[3] https://www.washingtonpost.com/opinions/2019/03/18/racist-terrorists-are-obsessed-with-demographics-lets-not-give-them-talking-points/?utm

[4] https://futurism.com/google-unveils-ai-learns/

[5] https://www.scmp.com/tech/big-tech/article/3004340/people-need-wake-dangers-ai-warns-hong-kong-professor-and-google

[6] https://www.vox.com/future-perfect/2019/2/15/18226493/deepmind-alphafold-artificial-intelligence-protein-folding

[7] https://www.billboard.com/biz/articles/news/record-labels/8504178/european-union-votes-in-favor-of-sweeping-copyright-reforms

The effects that networks have on people are statistical; for every individual who self-radicalizes there are many more who are merely made more irritable and paranoid (the diffuse forms of "fight or flight") than they would otherwise be. Researchers have detected an unprecedented level of "negative partisanship"[8], meaning that people no longer vote for anything, but against other groups of people; indeed when ideas or plans are at stake, there's an emerging new norm of "no to everything".[9]

Doesn't this sound like a world inhabited by people who don't feel the world wants them? It's a new universe of the lost.

The same companies that have trapped us in attention algorithms are also telling us that we'll be replaced. Is it any wonder that some of the trapped people "self-radicalize" online around the fear of being replaced?

The second most prominent story of the week in which I write is about plane crashes. Automation has been part of aviation for decades. In the past, it was often called "fly by wire" technology, and pilots were trained to use it like any other tool.

Something has changed. The new idea, apparently, is that automation is more like a creature than a tool, so pilots don't need to be trained to use it like any other tool.

Boeing added automation software to a new aircraft design but reports indicate that the pilots may not have received the training or resources necessary to assure that they could override this new kind of automation when a sensor was faulty.[10] Boeing have denied this, and investigations into the causes of

---

[8] http://www.stevenwwebster.com/negative-partisanship.pdf
[9] https://www.nytimes.com/2019/03/29/world/europe/brexit-theresa-may-democracy-chaos.html
[10] *https://www.nytimes.com/2019/02/03/world/asia/lion-air-plane-crash-pilots.html

the crashes following the software update are on-going[11], but I can't help wondering: If it weren't for the cult of AI, might the pilots have been better trained to understand how the new software worked and avoided the crashes and the death of hundreds?

We are often asked to fear AI because the robots of the future might wish to see us dead, but for me, this scenario shows us the true danger of AI. Believing in AI is the thing that could kill us.

How we integrate computation into our lives is the definitional challenge of our times. The underlying questions are ancient: How do we feel about ourselves? What is our meaning? Who gets the power? How can we overcome infighting to address our greatest challenges, like climate change? Those old questions are now about computers and networks. We must invent a new pattern of civilization in which we aren't using computers primarily to trick each other and pursue bizarre fantasies of building new gods.

Part Three: Is Anything Getting Better?

I have often been asked if I consider this book to have failed when an individual reads it but does not delete.

It could have been written in a different way. I could have covered the same points without challenging you to do something that you will probably not do. That way I would have hedged my bets. I wouldn't put myself or you at risk of a perception of failure.

It was the right risk to take. Challenging you to delete emphasizes that you do have personal responsibility in our era. You do have the potential to be more aware of your role via

---

[11] https://www.bbc.co.uk/news/business-47980959; https://www.seattletimes.com/business/boeing-aerospace/failed-certification-faa-missed-safety-issues-in-the-737-max-system-implicated-in-the-lion-air-crash/

platforms even when those platforms are opaque, controlled by others, and are designed to "engage and persuade" you in tricky ways.

No one can be perfect. We can't live in a way that perfectly moves the world as we wish it to move in every detail. We sometimes eat the wrong things; we don't make all the choices we could to reduce our carbon footprint, or all the choices that would support people who are at the wrong end of the injustices of our world. But awareness does contribute to gradual change. The more people are aware, the

easier it is for each individual to change, a little at a time. I've seen it happen in my lifetime with cigarettes, apartheid in South Africa, and many other issues.

Of course I knew that everyone wasn't going to delete their accounts; the combination of behavioral addiction with the grip of "network effects" (the way you depend on a platform you don't trust just because everyone else is there) is an unending plague.

But even so, a lot of people DID delete! While only the companies know for sure, there are estimates that about ten percent of Facebook users in the United States deleted in 2018.[12] What's more, an internet format that I praised in this book, podcasting, is exploding in popularity.[13]

How much of a difference did this book make? Our world is opaque; we are not allowed to know. That kind of information is only available to companies like Facebook and Google.

But at least thousands deleted their accounts after reading it. I know because a storm of them wrote to me, and I'm not easy to reach. (I must apologize for not writing back to everyone; it is impossible to do so.)

---

[12] https://www.techradar.com/news/nearly-one-in-10-us-facebook-users-have-deleted-their-accounts-survey-says
[13] https://www.edisonresearch.com/infinite-dial-2019/

To those who have deleted, I send congratulations and warmest wishes. You are the future. You are part of the reason our awkward species might survive.

Deleting has become reputable. There have been new studies of deleters; the evidence that deleting is good for you continues to grow[14].

Even so, deleters remain a minority. The addiction wave dominates.

And yet deleters have accomplished something wonderful. They have created a space for a conversation outside the addiction system. The way we talk about sneaky tech platforms has become more distanced and objective, though we still need to do better. But the very idea that people can and are deleting has broken through what used to be a barrier made of unchallenged assumptions.

For example, top engineers and scientists at the big tech companies have become vocal and public when they are displeased with company policies. The new wave of protests isn't always aligned with my point for view, but it often is. Either way, I applaud it. Silicon Valley is made of humans, and those humans are starting to take responsibility.

Government regulators are starting to understand the nature of the new beast and are becoming more confident. We will see if upcoming elections continue to benefit irritable and paranoid politics.

I'm ever more optimistic, but for the moment, truth is still losing. BUMMER politics has seen gains in places as diverse as Brazil and Sweden, and too many parents are still afraid to vaccinate their children. It's terrifying to me that optimistic young politicians like Alexandria Ocasio-Cortez continue to

---

[14] https://www.engadget.com/2019/01/31/study-says-quitting-facebook-improves-happiness/

depend on the same platforms that have brought ruin to previous waves of hopeful politics.

A fascinating new wave of positivity and invention has arisen in tech and design communities with the mission of inventing a post-BUMMER world.[15] A cryptocurrencies crash cleared out some of the get-rich-quick hucksters and brought to the fore the hopefulness that originally motivated inventions like blockchain.

The typical opinion piece about Facebook, Twitter, or YouTube has shifted tone. Opinion pieces now highlight the maladies these platforms inflict on the world, and often end with laments that nothing can change, because the problems arise from the business model. After all, even when Facebook does its best to reduce the horrors it amplifies, the effect is to ruin the moderators it hires.[16] You can't fix a poison factory by hiring an army of poison tasters. A poison tasting robot won't work either. Almost everyone finally understands that. The cliché conclusion has become a sad, knowing assertion that we'll be stuck with a darkened world forever.

I don't take these pessimistic stories as examples of defeat, but as progress. Soon enough, the writers will realize there's no reason to accept that the business model can't change. When that moment comes, there will be demands for change, and then the BUMMER world will start to dissolve into something better.

Some of the non-BUMMER platforms that have always been there are seeing expanded social roles that demonstrate a path forward; GitHub is a fascinating example.

This was not the only book that spurred change; other helpful books have appeared from writers like Mary Gray,

---

[15] Check out the participants in this conference: https://radicalxchange.org/

[16] https://gizmodo.com/report-facebook-moderators-are-routinely-high-and-joke-1832870719

Shoshana Zuboff, Roger McNamee, Sherry Turkle, Tiffany Shlain, Douglas Rushkoff, and many more, as well as a rising culture of technology criticism from many sources.

It has begun to feel like a race between tech platforms and thoughtful critics. Can we change course before humanity confuses itself to death through AI-powered deception?

We need to find a way back to reality, and the only way to do that is to have conversations that aren't mediated by technology that is financed and animated by third parties who hope to persuade us. We must fight to speak to each other outside of the persuasion labyrinth.

PS: Research continues to show that cats understand more than they let on because they are inner directed; they resist meeting the expectations of trainers.[17] There's still time to become a cat!

---

17 https://www.nationalgeographic.com/animals/2019/04/cats-recognize-names-dogs-pets/

THANK-YOUS

This book arose in an unusual way. After you write a book, you talk to journalists about it. When I talked to journalists about my previous book, which was about virtual reality, the conversation often turned to a different, immediately urgent topic. Social media was playing a role in making the world newly dark and crazy, and I was asked about that. This book arose from things I thought of to say when confronted. I must thank the journalists who forced this issue, including Tim Adams, Kamal Ahmed, Tom Ashbrook, Zoë Bernard, Kent Bye, Maureen Dowd, Moira Gunn, Mary Harris, Ezra Klein, Michael Krasny, Rana Mitter, Adi Robertson, Peter Rubin, Kai Ryssdal, Tavis Smiley, Steven Tweedie, and Todd Zwillich.

Thanks to Jerry Mander; this book's title is a tribute to his work.

Thanks to Kevin, Satya, and my many other colleagues at Microsoft for accepting a nonconformist in their ranks. That said, I am speaking strictly for myself. Nothing here represents a Microsoft point of view.

Our cats Loof, Potato, Tuno, and Starlight taught me how to not be domesticated, but not as much as the master teacher, my daughter, Lilibell. And of course thank you, Lena, my wonderful wife.

penguin.co.uk/vintage